Unseen-Unheard

Straight Spouses from Trauma to Transformation

by

Amity Pierce Buxton, PhD
and
R. L. Pinely

CCB Publishing
British Columbia, Canada

Unseen-Unheard: *Straight Spouses* from Trauma to Transformation

ISBN-13: 978-1-77143-069-2
Second Edition

Library and Archives Canada Cataloguing in Publication
Buxton, Amity Pierce, 1929-, author
Unseen-unheard : straight spouses from trauma to transformation /
by Amity Pierce Buxton and R. L. Pinely. – Second edition.
Includes bibliographic references.
Issued in print and electronic formats.
ISBN 978-1-77143-069-2 (pbk.).--ISBN 978-1-77143-070-8 (pdf)
Additional cataloguing data available from Library and Archives Canada

Publisher: CCB Publishing
British Columbia, Canada
www.ccbpublishing.com

Dedications

My deepest gratitude to Amity Buxton; dear friend, inspiration, visionary, and Founder of the Straight Spouse Network. Thank you for hearing me when no one else could. Thank you for helping me get up off my kitchen floor.

- R. L. Pinely

To the 20,000-plus women and men who have dared to speak up and seek help from the Straight Spouse Network over the past 21 years. May their examples inspire the 1,000's more who remain unseen and unheard.

- Amity Pierce Buxton

Contents

Introduction

Welcome to the voices of an invisible minority, women and men who are unseen and unheard, even though you see and hear us in your neighborhoods, at work, in the marketplace, in faith communities, at public events, and on and on.

If we're seen and heard everywhere, how come we are invisible?

We're the wives and husbands of husbands and wives who turned out to be gay, lesbian, or bisexual – or transgender, (from cross dresser to transsexual) – at some point in our marriages. Some of us learned through disclosure, others through discovery. Either way, being told or finding physical evidence, we all experienced profound shock until we were able to face and then unravel years, sometimes decades, of unknowingly living a life based not on truth but rather on innocent unawareness or denial, "white" lies, deliberate deceit, or, sadly, sometimes infidelity. To the outside world, our husbands' and wives' coming out drew attention and often applause, rightly so, for their courage. Indeed, many found support in their respective lesbian, gay, bisexual, or transgender communities. However, the devastating impact of that courageous act on us, their spouses, was overlooked, minimized, or misunderstood by outsiders, including professionals, especially in the straight community. After all, we're straight, right? Yes, yet being straight becomes an issue in our marriages and a "box" into which outsiders assign us. At the same time, there are also those of us whose spouses never dared admit being gay, lesbian, bisexual, or "trans," despite undeniable evidence. We, in effect, become ciphers.

Explanations for this lack of recognition or understanding of a straight spouse's experience are many. First, fear of rejection by family, of the partner's being discriminated against at work or in the community, or of negative effects on our children lead often to our keeping the secret within the immediate family as a private matter. Secondly, even if a straight spouse confides in someone, the listener usually has little grasp of his or her unique issues. Instead, some spouses are told, "Well, let him (or her) go. You're straight after all. Get on with your life." Others hear, "So how come you couldn't figure it out?" Third, little information about straight spouses or the complexity of mixed-orientation and trans/non-trans marriages exists in the public or professional arena, with the result that many if not most therapists or clergy do not comprehend the singular factors involved when a spouse comes out or is discovered. As a result, whether closeted by choice or minimized by friends, family, and professionals, many straight spouses cope alone with their concerns and emotions, an isolation that magnifies and escalates their confusion and pain. Some are fortunate enough to find other spouses with whom to share so that they can heal and transform their lives.

Thus this book – where a range of straight spouses tell their stories and describe key episodes or insights freely to an audience who wants to hear and understand what happened to them when they found out their spouses were lesbian, gay, bisexual, or transgender (LGBT) – what their major issues were, how they coped, and how their lives eventually turned out after this shattering experience. Most of the people you are about to meet found peer support groups and confidential mailing lists via the Straight Spouse Network, which provides safe places for spouses to express their feelings and ask sensitive questions with a community of peers who understand and therefore are able to help by sharing their own stories or simply listening with empathetic ears since they've "been there."

The stories and short "takes" come from a variety of sources: several spouse-initiated story collections over the past five years; individual stories published on the Straight Spouse Network web site: www.straightspouse.org (Straight Spouse

Network, 2006); several narratives collected expressly for this book; one public presentation; and stories and emails that appeared on mailing lists of straight spouses and mixed-orientation couples from 2005-2011, some of which were used in a recent research article about straight husbands, (Buxton, 2012).

The spouses come primarily from the United States and also from the UK, Denmark, Canada, Australia, and the Pacific Islands. When invited to have their stories included, all were honored and excited to have their voices heard. Even so, at the last minute, a number, including those whose stories were previously available in limited, private venues, found it too painful and frightening to have their stories heard in a public venue, particularly if their spouses or families were still closeted or they were members of faith communities in which being gay is deemed to be immoral and damnable. To protect the privacy of those whose voices are here, some names and identifying details and/or places have been changed.

Our selection and organization of stories and email excerpts were based on twenty-six years of research about and interaction with over 20,000 women and men, formerly or still married to LGBT partners. We organized them in an order that might help you better hear and see the whole picture of a straight spouse's struggle and also to focus on specific aspects that help reveal underlying dynamics of a spouse's journey. "Amity" sets the stage for the full gamut of the impact of disclosure, while "R. L." pinpoints particular issues leading up to and following a straight spouse's discovery. Following these complete stories, "First Cries" are literally early cries for help online as spouses face the daunting challenges that pop up right after finding out or encounter unexpected obstacles along the route. "Forging through the Fire" then presents complete stories of adversity experienced by straight wives and husbands, who narrate how they coped with such challenges; while "Turning Points" focuses on moments that made the difference between a spouse's stagnating in the forging mode or totally giving up and his or her bold shifting of course to resolve particular concerns and daunting dilemmas one way or another. "Tug of War" looks at alternatives that pull spouses in opposite directions and how their choices are made. Finally, "Now" captures where two spouses are in their journeys "right here, right now," having resolved their particular issues enough to feel like transformed persons, strong and confident that, although tomorrow may bring new challenges, they can handle them with greater self-assurance than they could have yesterday. Following our "Afterword," we have included a list of references for any of you who would like a more scholarly look at the straight spouse's journey and also information about resources for spouses and their families.

We co-authors, R. L. Pinely and I, hope you will look at and listen to these remarkable women and men with open hearts and minds and realize that their opinions about LGBT spouses or straight spouses are not ours but rather their own, born out of their particular experience and perceptions at the time they expressed them. Of most interest to us, their stories not only express and describe what happened to them and what they thought and felt about it, but also shed light on the roles played by the passage of time, each spouse's changing perspective, the impact of immediate experience, and the malleability of memory. These protagonists ask questions many of us have raised in other situations at one time or another: Did it really happen? Why didn't I do this, not that? And, in the end, what matters most?

A final note before you start reading. We invite you to put aside any definitions you might have about hope, unconditional love, marriage, success, and failure. As straight spouses, we have had to keep redefining who we are and what our lives are about, sometimes moment to moment, sometimes hour by hour, sometimes day by day. Preconceived ideas and social norms didn't and don't work for us.

For straight spouses, hope means anticipating the good, recognizing the positive, making improvements, and creating a different way of thinking about life or living it. Unconditional love means setting aside all expectations and perceptions of what we wish we had and, instead, looking at "what is" in reality.

For straight spouses, success and failure are not determined by whether or not we stay married. Divorce does not qualify as failure; neither does staying together indicate success. Our measure of success encompasses more than the marriage, rather the who of our lives as we live them, flexing, breathing, and, yes, sometimes standing still. We realize success as we experience inner peace and contentment, which we measure by our self-awareness, strength, understanding, and growth. We find success also in our continuous desire and willingness to try to discover what works. The only time we allow ourselves to own failure is when we don't trust ourselves enough to do what we think may work, whether moment to moment, hour to hour, or day to day.

It's really about perseverance. What works right here, right now, and what we do at this particular moment may not necessarily be our permanent solution. We aren't settling, and we aren't failures. The choices we make along the way and the options connected with them may not be optimal in the long run, but they're the best we have working for us right this minute. Choices that are difficult and, in hindsight, unwise are not failures, but rather opportunities to keep seeking the best way to move our lives one more step closer to a renewed life, one moment, one hour, one day at a time.

We hope that, wherever you are in your own journey, reading the stories will interest and also inspire you. We hope they might help you create a new inner strength and give you the determination to keep moving your life forward, no matter by how small a step. This book is really about the greater good – not just "straight spouses." It's about enlightenment, empowerment, and unconditional love. Our stories are not about being victims, unintended or not, but about being victors in our own lives.

Again, welcome to the unseen and unheard.

Chapter 1
Amity

Writing this memoir turned out to be unexpectedly painful. Reliving the pre- and post-disclosure years with my gay husband unearthed forgotten agony, anger, and profound puzzlement. The easy part was describing how working through the trauma strengthened and transformed me.

Will and I met at a mutual friend's party, late 1955, when I was teaching at San Francisco State and he was working for the US government. When he said he lived in Palo Alto and didn't like mowing his lawn, I made him a deal. Since I'd be at Stanford in the summer to do Ph.D. research, I'd mow his lawn if he'd drive me up to San Francisco on weekends for my dates.

When I arrived in Palo Alto, I called and Will picked me up. Before mowing began, we sat out on the lawn, drinking gin and tonics and talking about everything under the sun. Eventually, I did mow that evening, but, in the following days, never again. Instead, we played tennis, dined out, and went to San Francisco one weekend. He also let me use his car to get my driver's license. His trusting that I could do so in HIS car amazed me. I was also totally turned on.

The month over, I took the Greyhound to New York to finish my Ph.D. coursework at Columbia, living with my parents. Not hearing from Will, I began dating several men, turning down the proposal of one because of a history of mental illness and breaking my engagement with another after too many arguments over religion. Per my mother's advice, I wrote Will about the breakup, which he later said didn't surprise him since he knew I was the one he'd marry. After intense correspondence, a Thanksgiving weekend in his new Sausalito apartment, and more letters and calls, we married two and half years after we'd met.

We made a remarkable twosome, doing everything together evenings and weekends: tennis, remodeling old houses, dancing, going to art shows, the theater, and the ballet, and traveling, the ultimate of which was a trip around the world to distract me from not getting pregnant.

Just before our departure date, I discovered I was pregnant. My doctor said traveling would be fine as long as I checked into pharmacies each month for a urinalysis. So, laden with my multivitamins, off we went to New York in the red MGA Will had given me so I wouldn't have to carry groceries home. Storing the car in my parents' town, we sailed off on the Queen Mary.

After touring for several months in the car we bought in Stuttgart, Will became ill in Italy. By the time he was diagnosed in Spain, the doctor said he had to be hospitalized. Since I was six months pregnant, the decision was based on where we wanted our baby born, Madrid or Paris. We chose the latter, and I drove us 90 miles an hour up and over to Paris, where the doctors at the American Hospital in Neuilly-sur-Seine said that all Will needed was good home care. So I rented an apartment (second floor of a three story home) in Suresnes and began a six-months-long life as a French wife, marketing every day for nutritious food for Will, finding a sage femme and doctor for me, and visiting museums – we decided that both of us didn't have to forego Paris sights, just because one was ill – all giving me multiple opportunities to use my beloved French.

Peter was born three months after that. When he was three months old, we took off to finish our European trip, me nursing Peter with a bundle of disposable diapers on hand, before we three sailed back to New York and took off in the stored red MGA to drive westward, Peter cradled in a French laundry basket at my feet. Home in Sausalito, we found a one-bedroom apartment near our former studio apartment and then bought a house, where we watched with wonder our son grow, while continuing to speak only in French with him as I finished and then defended my dissertation back at Columbia.

In 1964, Phyllis was born. It was her turn to delight us, as we watched her grow in the remodeled fisherman's cottage that we'd bought, while renting out the other house. Here, a fairy tale family life began. We remodeled the basement into children's quarters, and Will created a goldfish pond next to the playhouse he'd built at the back of the rear garden.

By then, after several commercial jobs, Will was working again for the government. When Phyllis was three and a half, I returned to work. Volunteering in a pre-Head Start school in San Francisco led me to an opening in a project at San Francisco State to train teachers for desegregating schools. I then found a French public school in San Francisco which enrolled children as young as three-and-a-half. I left Phyllis off there on the way to work and then picked her up en route home, driving through Golden Gate Park. Soon, since Peter wasn't being challenged enough in public school, he joined Phyllis, and I found French families with whom both children could stay after school until Will or I picked them up. By then, to make sure their English was "correct," Will was speaking to them in English, making dinner table conversations quite interesting.

Our lives were full, fun, and busy with social activities and family trips up the coast, in Canada, and a return to France. When Peter was ten, we moved to a larger community with good public schools and a swim and tennis club nearby. In my work, our multiethnic team pioneered a Teachers' Center in San Francisco, where teachers learned hands-on activities to enable every student in desegregated classrooms to reach his or her potential. Before long, I was commuting to Oakland, where the Center had moved, while Will took early retirement and engaged in various projects including figure skating, swimming in the Bay, and travel to Japan and Latin America. To fit his new life, his wardrobe changed a bit.

As Peter entered his teens, becoming increasingly independent of us in all areas, Will seemed to withdraw and show the signs of depression he'd shown years before when a psychologist had diagnosed its cause as my energy, which I thereupon had toned down. This time, I found every kind of medical resource I could to help him reverse the withdrawal, from a specialist in bio-chemicals to the family doctor, who simply asked him if he was depressed. Since Will said he wasn't, the doctor reported to me that he wasn't. But I knew something was going on as he became more and more distant at home while still being a central raconteur at dinner with friends. Recalling how he'd grown up without much love in his family, I poured my love on him, but no longer did any gestures of intimacy come in return. He turned away when I kissed his cheek, saying I did it "out of duty." ("What?" I thought.) Even when dancing, we weren't in sync any more, even as he danced cheek-to-cheek with the wives of couples with whom we often went dancing.

After Peter left for college, Phyllis entered her teen years and became her own person, whom Will increasingly criticized. I became alternately the tigress mother defending her cub and fixer of my husband's ailments, while I poured out my agony about our distancing on page after page of my journal while I sipped white wine. When I finally saw a therapist to help me sort out the confusion and pain, she said she envisioned Will and me as interacting according to our ideal images of ourselves, not in the here and now. That image made me decide I needed to figure out what was real in my life. I grabbed every piece of information that might help, like a radio interview about the importance of moving one's own expectations of oneself to the top of the list.

By 1982, I knew I couldn't continue living in this reality and said to Will one night, as he worked at his desk in the bedroom, "I can no longer live with a stone wall. I'm going to move out."

Without a second's pause, he said, "No, the husband always moves out." As we talked further, he added, "I'm a prisoner of the past and a hostage to my future." (Once again, I thought to myself, "What?")

Will's leaving didn't happen overnight. A series of steps led to his eventual departure. First, I wrote him a long letter suggesting he take a trip to help lift his depression and that we'd be there when he came home. Travel had always revived him. Next, he decided that, once Phyllis graduated from high school, he'd move into the city condo that we'd just bought so we could spend the night after the theater or ballet rather than drive home across the bridge. Then, though I'd said I wanted us to tell the children about the separation together, he told Phyllis that he was leaving as he drove her to college and told her not to tell Peter.

The morning Will moved out, I kissed him good-by and wished him well as I left for work. In response, he said, "I was promised that if I did what I was supposed to do, I'd be happy. But I wasn't."

I went to the garage, feeling more sad and hurt than puzzled about his statement. When I returned home that night, the only signs of Will were gaps where the furniture he took had been. Over the following weeks, I opened curtains and blinds throughout the house, adding more light, and placed pillows here and there. One day, a bouquet of flowers arrived with a note: "Forgive me. My fate was stronger than my love." Whatever that meant.

We had no plans about what to do next. We kept in touch, celebrating holidays and birthdays as a family, while I continued teaching, writing, doing research, giving talks, and traveling in connection with teachers' center work (once giving a talk in French in Paris). During a birthday lunch for me at a restaurant near where we used to live, the two of us began to talk about our marriage. Will explained that his reason for stopping sex was my sexual shortcomings (rather than his not having enough energy for having more children, as he'd told me at the time). White anger rose up from my insides. More was said, angering me so much that I called for the check and said we had to leave.

On the way to his condo, we sat in silence. Once there, I exploded, shouting, "How dare you assume what I think? Why didn't you ask me? What else haven't you told me?" Exhausted, I finally went home.

Things calmed down for about a year, until I visited Will when he was recovering from minor surgery and under medication. "I've got something to tell you," he began.

Subconsciously recalling the thought I'd had when I'd noted his earlier wardrobe changes -- that he might be a latent homosexual -- I blurted out, "I think I know."

It was more than that. He proceeded to say that he was gay and had discovered that he was the very weekend of the Sunday evening he'd met me, had excommunicated himself when a priest confessor didn't after Will told him he was gay, and had jilted his lover to marry me.

Whether in relief or amazement, I burst out laughing. "We're better than a soap opera!"

Now I knew why our sexual relations had ceased, his attraction to me waned, and he had become depressed. Yet there were loose ends and other "why" questions. Will referred me to a support group for straight wives of gay and bisexual husbands and invited me to a brunch he gave at his condo so I could meet his gay friends. I really liked them. One, the Gay Fathers of San Francisco President, asked me to organize a panel of straight wives and husbands for one of their meetings.

By this time, I'd located three support groups for straight spouses in the Bay Area, from which I asked three other wives to join me on the panel. At the meeting, when we finished telling our stories, the fifty-plus gay dads in the room gave us a standing ovation, tears streaming down their faces. Because we weren't their wives, they could "hear" us. The President then asked me to run a support group for the dads, which I did for a year or so, resulting in a number of men's becoming able to resume communication with their wives and thereby see their children again. This success caused the President to suggest that I write a book so other gay dads could understand their wives. I agreed, knowing from my support groups that straight husbands, too, had to be included.

All this time, I thought our marriage might work now that I knew the problem. Will said, however, that if he came back, "The same thing would happen again." Then I thought it would work if he and his original boyfriend, whom I liked, got together. When I brought up the idea, Will said he was too monogamous. Yet, the idea wouldn't go away. Although I'd agreed to his request not to tell anyone about his being gay, including the children, I felt safe telling a professional friend at a conference about Will and my idea of a threesome. She pointed out some real life difficulties of having his boyfriend live in the same house. Seeing no more possibilities, I knew the marriage was over.

That summer, I returned to France to replenish my soul and recapture some of what we two had years before. The visit turned out to be strange though powerful. Yes, I absorbed Matisse and Picasso in Nice, but I also did some bizarre things, trying, I think, to prove that I was stronger than the situation. First, I climbed the steps all the way up the mammoth cliff from the Basse Corniche to the Grande Corniche in 90+ degree heat and humidity and, then, in Paris, deliberately jay-walked across a boulevard, weaving left and right through the helter-skelter flow of cars.

Once home, it was clear that divorce was the only option. I knew that was frowned upon by the Catholic Church but checked with a Paulist priest in San Francisco, who asked me simply, "Do you feel the marriage is over?" When I nodded, he said, "Then you are already divorced."

Will and I worked out details of a 50/50 divorce, while I burned the candle at both ends with a merry-go-round of work-related activities and dating until I was hospitalized with mononucleosis. Recuperating, I happened upon *Siddhartha* by Herman Hesse, which showed me the difference between being and becoming, the present moment and measured time. From there, I devoured books about Middle Eastern and Asian religions and philosophies, took courses in human sexuality and workshops in Native American traditions, and attended lectures on various theologies. My search for meaning went on and on to the point that I thought about joining another denomination so I could be a minister. That December, while Christmas shopping, I found myself at the door of a small church left from California Missions. Exhausted, I entered and knelt in the back. "I'm all alone," I murmured.

Then, a voice thundered, "I am here."

Startled for a moment, I then thought, "Of course. How did I forget?"

The divorce was final in 1985. By then, Will was living with the first of two partners, and I started placing and responding to personal ads. Through several respondents, I discovered what heterosexual sex was all about. My sexuality unleashed, I felt slightly off balance, which sent me back to my therapist, who helped me see I'd simply released the Amity who had been hidden. Yes, she had flaws, but she was reborn, whole, and new.

At some point, I realized I couldn't remarry in the Catholic Church unless our sacramental marriage contract was annulled. After researching the theology and history of marriage, I filed for a church annulment on the basis of "error of person" (no disclosure by my husband of his sexual orientation). The Tribunal granted it on a different basis, supported by Canon Law statements, one of which referred to "personality disorder." That annoyed me because it was not my reason for the annulment nor was it the nature of homosexuality. Will objected strongly, leading to a messy, costly, and lengthy legal event.

These church-related procedures and legalities wore me down so much that in desperation I called the Archdiocese to find someone to counsel me. All but the office staff person were off at their annual picnic, so I telephoned the local parish, where the priest on duty happened to be a Forgiveness expert. In fifteen minutes, over the phone, he talked me through three stages of forgiveness: ordinary, conditional, and absolute. For each, I was to discern and answer, "Yes" or "No." After saying "Yes" to the three, I found myself sobbing and feeling that a heavy burden on my shoulders had been lifted. The exercise benefitted me and had nothing to do with Will.

Meanwhile, Will came out to Phyllis, and she told Peter, so I felt free to call our son, saying, "I know that you know, so I'm not telling you." That opening gave Peter the freedom to talk about his feelings about his father's being gay, although he had to wait several years before Will told him. It was only after hearing it from his father himself that Peter really believed it.

By then, I'd taken early retirement to write *The Other Side of the Closet* and had met a man who shared my interest in spiritual, metaphysical, and conceptual realms as well as being a fellow writer and reader. After we dated for a time, I joined his Unitarian church, where classes in diverse theologies were held, and continued to go to Mass. On Valentine's Day, 1988, I moved in with him (to make sure he was straight). Life was full and became fuller as we back-packed, rafted down the Grand Canyon, and traveled to Southeast Asia, India, Latin America, Israel, Greece, and Southwest United States to immerse ourselves in those cultures and expand our understanding, a quest crowned by conferences on science and consciousness in Albuquerque. While, as in every relationship, we had our ups and downs, our physical/sexual spark stayed burning bright.

Will and I stayed in touch, called each other and sent birthday and holiday cards; and he sent birthday gifts to me until my new partner and I married in 1991. After that, we just exchanged cards for birthdays and Christmas and organized our lives separately, Will, reuniting with his family of origin, and I, joining my new husband's side of the family.

That same year, *The Other Side* was published and I was given the reins of a task force and a small national group that supported straight spouses of gay, lesbian, and bisexual persons. I combined them to create the Straight Spouse Network to provide worldwide peer support and research-based information to spouses in the same mixed-orientation marriage situation in which I'd found myself. Before I knew it, I was doing the research, conducting workshops, and giving lectures here and abroad. Soon, I expanded the network to include spouses of transgender and trans/non-trans couples. Early retirement went out the window, though this work didn't pay.

Fast forward ten years, when Phyllis called to report that Will had been hospitalized for cancer surgery and maybe I'd like to visit. By then, he had ended his second relationship. I recall the visit vividly because he said he'd looked out his window at the cityscape of tall buildings and thought it was the Twin Towers of 9/11. As he recuperated at home, I eased the children's daily checking in on him and traveled from Oakland to San Francisco every third day to visit, do errands, or have lunch. It was actually fun, because we hadn't lost our lively give-and-take of ideas and experiences. One day, as we walked down the street, I chuckled, thinking, "Me and my gay husband and straight husband -- and both with canes."

Early in 2002, Will called to tell me what a nice time he'd had with Phyllis a few nights before when they'd dined together to celebrate her birthday. Then, all of a sudden, the tone of his voice fell, echoing his former depression. I became concerned and, as usual, said something I thought could boost his spirits.

That was the last time we talked. Two days later, he passed away in his condo, without family or friends at his side. I was the Executor of his estate, and the children handled his physical belongings. We three, plus Will's brother, sisters, their spouses, and my husband, flew to Arlington National Cemetery for a ceremony with full military Honors to bury his ashes. Between tears and shaking, I half-smiled and said to myself, "One more gay military person is being buried here."

Will's death devastated me. In my earlier writing and speaking, I'd declared that, compared to having a spouse die, it was harder for straight spouses who divorced because, as they co-parent, they have to deal with constant tangible reminders of the partners they'd lost. Now, I realized that death in its finality was worse. Sobbing sessions persisted for more than a year until just sadness lingered whenever I thought of Will.

Ultimately, my pain from not knowing Will's secret, the tumult of tackling unanswerable questions, and the torment of seeing damaging effects on gay men and lesbians who married persons of the opposite sex as the "right thing to do" – and also on their straight spouses – tore apart everything I believed. A kind of metaphysical, spiritual force grew inside me, sustaining me as I worked through the dilemmas and widened my perspective to see life as "both/and" rather than "either/or." Out of the trauma, a new Amity emerged, scarred but stronger, one who puts her needs, wants, and values first; who understands why Will hid his identity and believes he loved her as much as he could; and who, though upset at having lived someone's else's script, works passionately to change societal and religious attitudes that condone only opposite-sex marriage and condemn gay and lesbian persons and same-sex marriages.

This past year, my second husband passed away after an agonizing battle with cancer, during which he still lit up when he saw me and often opened his arms, inviting me to sit on his lap. I was with him and felt his last breath. The scattering of his ashes in San Francisco Bay put me face to face with the finality of death once again. However, this time, rather than devastation, I simply feel alone with an empty space beside me.

"What Amity will emerge next?"

Chapter 2
R. L.

So, do you stay? Divorce? No one wants divorce. How do you know if or when it's the right choice? It's an internal gauge, and it's uniquely yours. For me, divorce was sadly inevitable. My ex-husband is gay. He was unfaithful for years. I prayed that he would change, that he would accept God in his life, and that *that* commitment would bring him back to the vows he made at the altar. *That* didn't happen.

It took me eleven years of hanging on to hope, examining my faith, and living in a very dark closet before I filed for divorce; eleven years of empty promises, rejection, loneliness, gas lighting, excuses, coping with his active infidelity, and my own denial.

Until very recently, I was not emotionally well grounded enough to write this. Why? My story is raw. When I was married, I put my husband and his worldly desires in front of my commitment to God. It was the biggest mistake I could have ever made. Those years were very, very dark years.

I feel conflicted writing this now because I allowed my then husband's reality to compromise my Christian values; therefore, writing the truth is very difficult. I was a much different person back then. Long before my son was born, I identified with the world, believing I was going to salvage my marriage which, in reality, was only hanging on by a thread.

I coined a term I call "The Gerbil Wheel," which describes the very dysfunctional cycle of what we experience, what we know, and how we continue to live with "it" and cope. My ex-husband was never emotionally invested in our marriage. He did what he thought he needed to do to get by, and the only time exactly

he bothered to care was when he was at risk of losing his very comfortable hiding spot.

We are six years post-divorce and, not only is he not out, he sought a beard *before* I left our marital home and he's had her in his life ever since. He found her on a dating site. She's wonderful, much older, very sweet, and she adores our son. My heart aches for her. They aren't married.

What's a beard? A beard is a woman whom a gay man seeks to make it apparent to the world he's heterosexual. She's a place to hide and nothing more, neither girlfriend or wife. Neither is preferable, since using someone is just wrong; however, the legal implications of doing so while married can be much more devastating.

What have I learned? I learned that Christ transforms us. There's no looking back. The only thing I can do is slowly take steps forward from here to live each day, striving to do His will and striving to live the life He has planned for me. Maybe you will read this and think to yourself, "Hypocrite!" Maybe you will read this and feel empathy, loss, or heartache. Maybe you will share my pain. I can tell you that Psalm 103:12 speaks to my heart, and Isaiah 41:10-13 makes me feel safe.

So, what was my Gerbil Wheel? My gerbil wheel spun and spun when I'd catch him "in the act" or find things: walking in on his sexual indiscretions while looking at gay porn sites, finding his "toy" stash, finding soiled and stained "trophy" underwear (4 sizes larger than his own) in his dresser drawer or something simple as receipts from a weekend away with his boyfriend when he'd said it was a business trip. When he'd get caught, all the activity stopped abruptly and a new super hero arrived on the scene in our house.

He became super husband, super church man, super dad…super this and that. Usually, it took a month or so and he'd slowly return to the late nights, weekends away, texts, emails, and passwords on everything. Funny how, just as soon as he would lift all the passwords on all the technology, our computer would crash or his phone would somehow find its way into the pool. Go figure! Another gerbil wheel—ready to spin, and it did the last eleven years of my marriage. There was a breaking point.

A Leopard Doesn't Change His Spots…

I never had a problem loving my uncles unconditionally. They've been together for 46 years. They were out early on to their families when they found each other. They are devoted to one another, completely monogamous, and deeply in love to this day. In many respects, they are and have been better role models than my own parents.

My problem is with liars, cheaters, deceivers, gas-lighters, passive-aggressives who consciously care about only one thing: themselves, leaving in their wake an aftermath of destruction and devastation. My ex-husband is a deeply closeted gay man. He does everything hurtful possible to create distance between himself and anyone who gets too close. It's all so pathetic. The years of infidelity have caught up to him.

* * *

How did it start—this gerbil-wheel turned nightmare? It was 1990. I'd just come home from living in Rome for the summer and was cynical at best. A friend of mine introduced me to Max.

My first impression wasn't "WOW," it was "Hmmm, he's really nice." After overcoming cynicism and letting myself be completely vulnerable, I fell very much in love. He came from a good Catholic family. He had a sharp sense of humor and, very early on, we seemed to enjoy the same things and we laughed often. Early on, we shared a secret glance that could make the world stand still. We finished each other's sentences. Dating was fun. We traveled, had a circle of friends, and did all the things that most couples do to learn about one another. We were comfortable with each other. We were like a favorite pair of slippers. We didn't have the initial catch-your-eye-stop-dead-in-your-tracks attraction.

I always thought he was quirky and wanted so much to put my finger on it. There was a distance between us I couldn't figure out. When most couples naturally expressed intimacy like holding hands, you would have thought our hands were two magnets with the same ends being forced together. He repelled. When I look back on it, he did what he thought was expected. He wanted to look the part. We were engaged the following year and married in 1992.

The orange crate years, as I call them, are supposed to be the days you look back on as you celebrate sweet memories in your "golden years." I sit here telling you my story now as a single parent remembering ski trips, scuba trips, cruises, church functions, and holiday parties. I don't remember my husband. He was transparent. I guess I'm not quite sure what we would have had to look back on. Our marriage was stoic at best.

Because he was so focused on living a life outside of ours, there was no playful intimacy between us, no laughter, and no connection. It was baffling. I was confused because, very early on in our relationship, he seemed genuinely interested in wanting to please me. Evidently, he was saving all that for his boyfriend, the one true connection he needed and desired. I was nothing more than a place to hide.

And because he was so detached, the need for intimacy was mine alone. I was the one initiating and learned how to be selfish to be "satisfied." Nothing affected him emotionally. He was physically isolating. I always had to initiate holding hands, insist on sitting on the couch together, and touching in bed. It was always me.

I never felt like I ever met his needs. I never felt like I was ever enough. It took me years to stop trying to please him, to wake up and be selfish enough to realize I was living in the worst state of loneliness and isolation I'd ever known because *my* needs were never met. I was so focused on how to make him happy I never once thought it wasn't me. I was so focused on how to make him happy that I neglected my relationship with God.

Our ranch style rental wasn't much to speak of, but it was home, and our twin Golden Retriever puppies and our two Siamese cats found it adequate as well. How did I discover?

It was 1995. We were D.I.N.K.s, Double Income No Kids, and, with Max working Saturdays, admittedly I eventually looked forward to that time and claimed it as my own. I was doodling on a desk calendar while waiting to get online in the early days of "dial up" and saw writing through the bottom of the page. Claw-like scratch marks didn't hide "BIG WEDGE," "YOUR HAMMER," and "ROCKHARD4U." He excused it away with telling me about his curiosity of swinging and wanting a threesome, while showing me the webcam he bought.

Desperate for attention and intimacy, I spent the first few months with him on his terms, then mine. I didn't want to be with anyone else and was devastated knowing my husband didn't feel the same way. I turned my back on God, compromising my dignity and my value system. When I look back on it, swinging was the closest he could get to a naked man without being obvious. Even with a set of rules, I felt filthy. It was degrading, disappointing, and lonely at best. It confirmed that my husband didn't want me and wasn't interested in me. I refused to do it anymore, and he got angry. So, what little hand holding we did, what little he sat on the couch next to me or laid next to me in bed, came to a screeching halt.

Maybe it didn't help that I had his login name and password to a gay dating site. I left his profile in full view for him to see when he got home. There he was in all his glory, my then-husband, profile and package available for any man who wanted to "shop" for him. I tried to talk to him about it and again he brushed it off and told me I was absurd for thinking he wanted to be with a man. He told me it was all in my head. Within a week, he had his own user page on our computer and it was password-locked; inaccessible.

He started actively finding a social life which included dating and a new circle of friends. He sought gay married men because they were a "safe" hiding spot. He didn't touch me for a year and half. Looking back on it, I want to believe he didn't want to expose me to disease, so it was easier for him to neglect me, thinking I'd get to the point that I'd reject him and lose interest in him. It didn't work. The distance only made me want him more and desire intimacy more. It was a black hole. What it did do was send me to a therapist in a very dark state of depression.

It was the beginning of the end for my marriage and the introduction of gas lighting, denial, depression, and anxiety. Infidelity took on a whole new meaning. It was the first time I'd sought spiritual counsel from our priest.

It was our 7th Anniversary and I realized, for him, he had more than an itch to be with a man. My only thought, hope – "I hope he will change." During those first seven years, we'd saved enough to build a home in a lovely golf community. You would have thought by now I would have peeled the onion and shed my denial skin. Nope. See, until now, I convinced myself that all his goings on were "underground" and behind closed doors. Denial was easy because I didn't have to look at "it." Gay wasn't completely in our home yet.

When did I open my eyes and really accept that my husband was a deeply closeted gay man? It was football Sunday, when we were in the family room, inhaling hot wings and watching the Giants play. It was a soft drink commercial, the one with women in the skyscraper office looking down on construction workers. The pinnacle point was when a woman wipes the sweaty can with her finger tip and licks the dew off the soft drink can, while watching the men. For whatever reason, I was watching Max as much as the commercial. He got rock hard watching the men, and I realized, at that point, I feared the worst. I had to accept that we had more in common than I wanted to believe. We both wanted, desired, and needed a man.

It was more than I could handle. I went back to church to see my priest. You know something in your life has to change when your Vatican I vintage priest says, "You gotta get the hell out of there!" Every time I went to Mass with or without Max, he'd pull me aside and ask me, "Why are you still with him?"

I was living in Dante's Inferno. There are no words to describe the isolation and loneliness. There wasn't anyone to talk to. My husband abandoned me emotionally and physically. Who would possibly believe me? Max was "Mr. Joe Shmoe, everyday American guy." On the outside looking in, I found out years later, our neighbors always referred to us as "Mr. Roger's Neighborhood." When we had our son, we evolved to the "Cleavers."

As the years passed, so did our financial situation. We roller-coastered in and out of unemployment. Max was in and out of relationships. At one point, he lost his job for almost two years. He took side jobs that paid cash. When I look back on it, I realize he found work through his gay friends and he delayed looking for work in the traditional 9-5 corporate setting. He had the best of both worlds: his male sexual encounters (some of whom he invited over while I was at work) and side cash, and the wife at work bringing in the primary income.

I'd come home and he'd have unemployment applications printed out, "proving" his search. He'd blame his isolating behavior on a fake depression, claiming that being out of work was so hard on him, when in reality he was cherishing the alone time to find a partner and begin the life he had wanted since he was a child. When I was home, I was an intrusion and interrupting "his" time.

By 2001, with "passive-aggressive" in high gear, he needed more emotional control. He was tired of me needing to know "more." Spyware arrived on the scene. Ironically, he started tracking my computer usage. I didn't care. I had nothing to hide. He still had a lock on his cell phone and his user page of our family computer. He had passwords on everything. Max had successfully (so he thought) built a fortress around himself and his gay life. He even tried to create distractions.

He purposely eyed the woman next door. He purposely made very close friendships with women at work and left me in the worst state of loneliness I'd ever known. He made me believe it was all me, when, in fact, he needed to distance himself at any cost. At this point, he was actively unfaithful. I remember when he and his first boyfriend broke up, he was moody and even threw tantrums and fits when he couldn't find something he was looking for. You would have thought the world had come to an end. I was seeing a therapist, taking meds for depression and anxiety, and it was the first time I told him I wanted a divorce. He didn't take me seriously. I'd been shut completely out of his life.

He came and went independently, kept late hours, was gone most weekends. Anything we did as a couple was out of obligation, and he made it painfully clear that it was inconvenient. Again, I brought up divorce, telling him, "You aren't happy. I don't meet your needs, and I won't ever be able to." Knowing I have a deep faith, he pulls out a Bible and shows me where God says divorce isn't acceptable.

My reality? OK, you're gay. I HATE the fact you won't talk to me. I cannot cope with the physical nor emotional isolation and loneliness. We're married for nine years, together for eleven years, and you can't tell me what I already know anyway? You have a boyfriend. You have a box of "toys" in our master bedroom closet, and the tubes of lube change weekly! You have hook-up texts and conversations with your boyfriend about when you'll see each other next and how you can't wait. You can't have an open conversation in our home when your phone rings. You lock yourself in the office to use the computer. You masturbate to gay porn sites. You invite men into our home, have sex in our master bedroom, and then pretend you've been looking for work all day? You have trophy underwear in your drawer? OK! I get it! You're gay! You don't want me! Can't you at least talk to me about it instead of making me feel like hell every moment of every day?

With each passing year, I tried to talk about divorce, knowing I didn't meet his needs. Being that I was a very young and uninformed Christian, I believed Max when he'd bring me a

Bible and show me the scripture where God says divorce is not acceptable. But what about infidelity? Adultery? Lying? He didn't have anything to say about that. Was it my own denial? My own fear? Probably. I bought his Bible bit and stayed. We shifted our focus to children and raising a family. Now, I see he wanted me to have a distraction. I was too close to home for him. I knew too much and saw too much. He needed to do something if he was going to keep his closet, and he did keep his closet. We kept up the illusion of family well among what few friends we had.

By 2002, our only child, our son, was born. He became my world. Max insisted I go back to work after the usual three month maternity leave. I couldn't do it. I tried. I tried to leave our son at day care and couldn't do it. God has a way of working things out. Much to Max's chagrin, I insisted on shifting assets to give us some greater financial freedom and we did. I was a stay-at-home mom and living every moment of the teachable moment for our son.

Nothing changed in the marriage. I tried to talk to Max. Every time I brought up gay, I was shut down; so then the discussion turned to his same Bible "bit," telling me what he thought God said about divorce, while my own priest was showing me scripture that told me there are conditions for divorce, showing me what God wants for me and my life, and telling me that I won't realize any of it married to Max.

Then, one night, instead of the usual four-course meal, Max came home to an empty house with a divorce packet sitting on the dining room table. I had taken our son out for the day to play and then made plans for dinner at my parents. I came home late to find him pacing in the kitchen, asking me over and over if this is really what I wanted. There was no hesitation. "Yes," I remember saying, "the sooner the better, really." Our son was just two.

He threatened to take our son away from me. I knew better and refused to allow his irrational fear tactics to control me. I stood on solid ground, and Max realized he needed to switch gears. When he realized I was still serious and that I wasn't going to change my mind, he changed his MO and begged me to stay, telling me I don't deserve him and then promising to make the next 40 years of my life the best I'd ever know. If I could just erase the entire past and start over, he'd show me. Well, he showed me all right.

I sent him to our 10x12 guest bedroom for months and let him back in our room on his birthday. We weren't intimate. He went through all the motions of marriage for a while: being home on time, going to church with me again, seeming to care. It was all so very sterile. There was no real desire for me, and there was no real desire for him to want to be a family. He was doing what he thought he had to do and nothing more. By this time, his other life was in full swing. He took calls only out on the patio or in the backyard. He would use the computer only with the office door locked. Our home was nothing more than purgatory for him. He couldn't wait to leave the house in the morning, and he was always late coming home. He was working again, and I was a stay-at-home mom. I was seeing our priest almost weekly to gain strength and perspective.

What was the end? It was January 2006. I called Max on his way to work asking him to remember an MD appointment for our son. He answered "What?" in a tone that let me know that not only was I unwelcome, but an intrusion. I hung up. He called back. I hung up on him. I knew he was making plans that had nothing to do with me, nor our son. With a few calls to "friends," I knew he was making plans with his boyfriend. In less than five months, he'd broken his promise. It was over. I was having a nervous breakdown that morning, called my neighbor to take our son to play with her son for a while, and called PFLAG (Parents and Friends of Lesbians and Gays).

PFLAG didn't have resources for me; however, they referred me to a woman in California who was from the Straight Spouse Network. I have no idea how I dialed. When she answered, I was sobbing so hard, I couldn't breathe. She listened for hours. I only realized after hanging up at almost noon I had called

California. This woman, Amity, picked up her phone at 7:00 am, heard my cry for help, and gave me strength to look beyond the whirlwind moment in which I was barely surviving. She was my anchor and my lifeline.

Knowing I just couldn't do this anymore, I set out many new things for Max to find in his life when he got home: his clothing and toiletries were moved back into the guest bedroom with a note. He said nothing and accepted that fate. He never asked to come back into the bedroom. He never argued. He no longer had a wife that cared about marriage, only divorce. There were no more dinners, no more sentiments, no more anything. I was done. From that day on, he found out that I would no longer speak about anything having to do with salvaging nor repairing our marriage. It was only about what needed to be done to create the life that our son and I deserved. In my eyes, he had had eleven years to talk about gay, to open up, to go to counseling, and he refused. I was nowhere closer to the truth than I was back in 1995 when I first discovered; and, at this point, knowing the truth wouldn't give me a reason to stay. It would fuel the argument for divorce further. There was nothing left for me to give and nothing left for me to hear. He broke the last promise he'd ever make.

I pieced together the resources, hired an attorney, and filed on the grounds of irreconcilable differences. The entire process took five months. Why did I file claiming just irreconcilable differences? Gay is about Max, not me. There are consequences for every decision he has made, and he has to live with that every single moment of his life. I don't think there's a judge in the world that could impose a greater punishment nor tougher sentence.

For me, divorce was not about degrading or embarrassing Max, but about empowering myself and setting my own soul free to live the life that I deserved. What good is all the heartache and emotional upheaval of dragging "evidence" into divorce? Every moment you spend in an attorney's office is associated with a very heavy price tag. No attorney can erase time, heal wounds, nor figure out monetarily "the cost of loss." For me, divorce was about prioritizing my needs, rising above, and moving my own life forward.

Once the final hearing was over, I had to dust off my resume, find a career again, and find a place for my son and me to call home. Due to economics, I was forced to stay in the marital home for months after the divorce. It was a horribly stressful time. When my son and I moved, I left everything behind.

So, what's next?

I have spent the last six years with a spiritual GPS (God's Personal Street map). I've been looking for me, and I continue to find Him. I spend a lot of time praying that He will direct my path. Even with GPS programmed for His will, I still hear "recalculating" every now and then as the path I choose and the one He has for me are very different. I find I'm often at crossroads, which test my faith. I'm often in new territory, traveling on uncharted roads; and yet, I'm very much at peace. I found a church home, bought a home, and pursued my passion of writing.

The greatest challenge for me was to stand on my own two feet and independently create a new life in such a way that I have an entire new future. I was asked to take over as owner of an online support group which reaches out to over 3,000 women in membership, who actively post or passively receive emails. I am blessed to have the opportunity to give back what so many gave to me at a time when life was so devastating.

At the divorce, I was buried and non-existent. I had to break out of old molds. A dysfunctional marriage, motherhood, and work defined me. Now, God defines me; motherhood, family, friends, and a rekindled romance are all secondary.

The two years following the divorce for me personally were filled with heartache as I tried to adjust to my new life definition, "divorced." I had so much loss, and I owned my son's loss. I thought I had to be "Supermom" to protect him from the reality of the visitation schedule and had to overcompensate for him being away from Mommy when he was so young. It was very hard balancing what I thought was important: the need to provide a fulfilling life for my son and the need to make ends meet. When I look back on it now, I see that I put a lot of unnecessary pressure on myself. I've relaxed a lot since then.

I have no regrets. When I was married, I made the most of whatever else I had in my life to make up for what was missing. In so many ways, I'd never known such loneliness; however, it taught me that inner peace and contentment do not come from this world. I rediscovered my relationship with God, volunteered and taught at church, and relied on my faith to get me through.

Admittedly, I could have gotten out long before our son was born and didn't because I was comfortable and couldn't wrap my head around gay enough to figure out what to do. We had a good lifestyle, nice house; we traveled. There was no obvious abuse. The entire outside world saw a happy couple, while inside? Well, you know. I was unseen and unheard for eleven years. I didn't tell anyone for a very, very, very long time. I suffered, as so many do, alone.

Someone recently asked me, "If your ex came out, what would do?" Well, that's easy. I'd hug him and invite him and his boyfriend over for dinner, and life wouldn't skip a beat. Gay isn't news to me. Honesty? Now, that would be worth celebrating! He came close to coming out only once. After I had filed, he was lying on the couch with another "sinus infection" in the midst of another depressive afternoon. He said, "You know, it's not like I'm going to jump out of a closet," to which I replied, "I'm not looking for you to jump out of a closet. I'm looking for honesty." That was the last he ever broached the subject.

Would it surprise you if I told you I'm blessed for having walked through the fire? I can look back and be thankful, recognizing God's hand at work in my life. Had I never known such loneliness, pain and loss, I would have never been able to recognize nor be ready for how He would work in my life. Had I not felt like I lost everything, I would never have been able to realize nor understand how much there was to gain through Him. When we live in the world and for the world, we become the world. I have come to realize that my life is not meant to be in this world, but worldly enough to be a testimony and worldly enough to share how God works and to let others know that faith and hope are not just essential elements, they manifest themselves when we have inner peace and when we are content, regardless of place or circumstance. How on earth can you find inner peace when you know divorce is imminent and you have children? You just want to get out from underneath it all, but also you ask yourself, “Should I stay for the sake of the children?”

If your heart is wrenching and the tears won’t stop, know that you’re not alone. I can’t tell you what’s right for you. I can only tell you that I weighed the pro’s and con’s, too. I had to ask myself if it were important to stay married for the sake of our son. For me the answer was clearly, “No.” I did a soul search and asked myself this very question, “Is it better to raise our son in a two-parent home where he will grow up learning how to tolerate depression, angst, stress, and lies or is it better to raise him in a single parent home where he has a chance to realize joy, contentment, and peace?” Again, the answer, for me, was clear. I can tell you from my experience, children are resilient; and, no matter what the hardship, as long as Mom is ok, they will be ok. I noticed in the very early days after the divorce that our son “owned” my stress. On my emotionally difficult days, my son would display an array of behaviors from clingy restlessness and tantrums to anxiety and hyperactivity.

My son is still hyperactive. He is calmer since I’ve changed to a job which has hours suited to his schedule. I took a huge risk after a health issue and dropped out of mainstream corporate America. That extra time has built a new level of security he never had before. I feel like a stay-at-home mom again. I had so many fears about money but now rely on my faith to know God provides. He has done so over and over again. My priority is raising my son and spending quality time with him while he’s young, giving him as much as I can. Every child deserves sweet memories of youth.

Is there a silver lining? Well, yes. The good news is that Max loves his son and enjoys him very much.

I read all about kids and divorce. I focused on the spiritual and emotional well being of my son, and, because of this, he transitioned well. I continue to spend a lot of time counseling him, not smothering him or spoiling him. I spend time answering the tough questions, giving simple answers. I give him honesty, not details.

Shortly after our move, my son, who was just 4, asked me a question, "Mommy, why aren't you and Daddy married anymore?"

"Son, Mommy and Daddy aren't married anymore because Daddy broke God's law," I answered genuinely.

"Which one?" he asked, knowing all Ten Commandments.

"That's between Daddy and me."

He looked around our new home and, after a few moments, looked at me and said, "It must have been pretty bad because we live here now."

"Yes, Son, it was." Then I hugged him and counseled him, explaining, "It doesn't mean that God doesn't love Daddy. God loves us all and wants us to accept Him in our hearts, and He wants us to learn all we can about Him. Daddy can ask for forgiveness and be forgiven. Daddy needs to go to God to do that. There are consequences for breaking God's law." I offered this with the deepest desire for honesty and yet simplicity.

My son didn't skip a beat. Off he went to his playroom. I felt that the simplest answer is the best answer.

Following the divorce, I did everything I could to create a new "normal" for my son. I made sure he had a structured routine. I planned regular play dates with familiar friends, insisting on visits with family on both sides and a sense of wholeness even though we were no longer whole. It gave him security at a very insecure time. I put a calendar in his room and, because he was just learning to read, color-coded the visitation schedule so he would know what to expect. I put pictures of my ex and our son's cousins in his room on his dresser, and I made a special “daddy pillow” and put it on his bed. It was a simple page protector with a picture of my ex, which I “sewed” onto the front of the pillow, literally using needle and thread. I'm sure there was an easier way. I always want my son to know that his father is a very important person in his life. I don't allow my biases to shadow the potential relationship he will have with his father. I told myself, “If anyone is going to ruin a relationship between our son and his father, it'll be his father.” No matter how hard, I always made sure he made his father holiday cards, birthday cards, etc. I found it's imperative to give losses closure and to look ahead for the sake of our son.

I also found that closure comes from within and without. It comes from within me and my being able to forgive myself, accept the past, and take steps forward slowly. The most important thing I did for myself was to spend time alone, focused on my faith. I had to “do the work.” For me, it was the only way I could recognize and understand my needs and gain the useful tool of discernment. Even though I was divorced and away from the dysfunction of our marriage, I still carried old survival skills: old habits, dysfunctional coping skills, and poor decision-making skills.

Closure came from without, too. It came without a price tag. It came without looking back, without regret, without emotional encumbrances, and without stagnation. You know, if my husband came out, it would be a horrible case of being addicted to pain: the burning desire to know more, his lies, my “evidence,” more lies, all in the name of what? Wanting the truth? The reality is that whether he was “in the closet” or “out,” I would never, ever get the entire truth. After 11 years of torment, I got off my own “addicted to pain” gerbil wheel. I got to a point where I just accepted that what I knew was enough and that pursuing more would only cause deeper heartache. It's that heartache at different points in my marriage that paralyzed me. I didn't want to be paralyzed anymore. I didn't want to stagnate after the divorce. I didn't want the whirlwind of confusion. I needed to be able to make important decisions. I see stagnation as death. If I stagnated after the divorce, I would have had to go to the funeral home, pick out my coffin, and find someone to say my eulogy. Actually, stagnation is worse than death. If I were dead, at least my spirit and body would have a resting place. There is no resting place for the mind, body, or soul when you stagnate.

So, what's my best insight? I realized that I don't owe anyone an explanation of who I am or what my life is like. I just seek God with all my heart. My life isn't perfect, and I don't always make the right choices. I do my best. What echoes over and over? "Be still," "Wait," and "Do everything decently and in order." Romans 8:28 pretty much sums it up for me. I learned I had to do the work alone to find me again and, in doing so, I found the love of my life. There is hope.

Someone asked me, "Did you ever think you'd fall in love?" The answer is, "No." I didn't intend to nor did I want to. I saw myself as a single parent raising my son. And then, I met the man who would change my life. I had to work through many ghosts, insecurities, and a lot of baggage to commit to a serious relationship. Early on, I was angry and on an out of control emotional roller coaster. Although I was no longer in the trenches of TGT and all that dysfunction, I still had old coping mechanisms and survival skills. I knew if I jumped too quickly, if I wasn't well equipped, I'd just crash and burn. I just knew better than to get involved too soon. I knew I wasn't ready. Think of it this way, would you use a tattered parachute to jump from a plane? I knew I couldn't possibly give myself to another completely until I felt I was whole. Ok, I know what you're going to ask, "But, will I ever be whole ever again?" My question back to you is this, "Were you ever?" Consider that the most profound growing we do is born out of the pain, realization, and acceptance of the adversity in circumstances in which we find ourselves.

Chapter 3
First Cries

Discovery? Disclosure? It's a journey through hell. The flags are often so far and few between that it can take years for us to really put together the puzzle of same-sex attraction or transgenderism.

Whether we're engaged, newlyweds and pregnant, or married for 37 years, within those first moments of finding out, we're paralyzed. If we reach out, we proceed with caution, fearing the unknown, but desperate to find someone whose words and guidance can anchor us through the storm, moment to moment. These are our first cries. Some are passionately raw views and some are muted and subdued, in which the straight spouse gives you a mere crack in the closet door to look through, as though testing the waters to see if anyone may really be listening. The fortunate have individuals in their lives they can tell and lean on for support. Then there's the rest of us. Most of us remain unseen and unheard for years, and we suffer neglect, rejection, and loneliness in silence.

I, R. L., often think of our pain, the emotional price tag, as a lava flow. Our surface is deeply scarred, thick, crusty, and imperfect, but we seem to be very solid. Underneath that scarred surface are our wounds, raw and gaping. They seep and burn their way into new emotional crevices, ripping open old wounds which bleed and heal again. It's forever changing the very fiber of who we are. I don't think we're ever stable, not after what we experience. The emotional foundation upon which we need to rely for stability is in constant motion. At a moment's notice, an emotional eruption can occur and a new flow slowly creeps its way into our soul. Never once should anyone underestimate the pain or the devastation it can cause at a moment's notice. It's here at the lava flow that we begin to understand the cost of loss. Listen to the first cries of some of us as we face pending losses.

* * *

What is it with me? I seem to go 2-3 weeks and I feel ok. Then I wake up, and I have anxieties, panic attacks. I feel like screaming and running like hell. Nothing has changed. As far as I know, my husband hasn't done anything except not have sex with me or any type of intimacy. I'm on a roller coaster. We don't have sex. I feel empty. I try to focus on the kids and work, but that doesn't work anymore. What do you all do when this happens?

* * *

It kick-started with a number of crushing revelations from my wife, including how lonely she's felt in our relationship for so long and has no desire to live out the rest of her life feeling lonely. She said she drank wine at night with me not to be festive but to quell that loneliness, that she's felt this way for years, etc. This morning, she was almost in tears as she revealed how I put work in front of her too many times to count and that she has long experienced "too much of not enough."

I'm the sole proprietor of my business. She's correct that I focused much of my time and attention on work. Part of my manic focus was wanting to provide for my family, part was sheer fright at making sure I could keep myself employed, project after project. I've always been generous with my income. I've given significantly to a number of charities year after year, paid for my step-daughter's car and college graduation, covered our vacations, major household expenses, and dinners out, and on and on. I never worried about covering so many costs and expenses. I didn't care. My money was "our" money.

I didn't have a hint of the "loneliness" factor. I had too many happy experiences with her, too many cards expressing how much she loved me and words telling me how she looked forward to spending the rest of her life with me, too many indicators that she was NOT feeling this way. Apparently, her anger was buried and she's been traumatized by this. (She revealed she secretly cried.) Was hinting at it once or twice over the years enough? Should there have been a crisis where we rolled up our sleeves and got counseling to talk about it all? Or was I stupid to not have noticed something – an ineffective mind-reader? I don't want to blame my wife, but I'm having the hardest time putting 100% of the blame on me.

The collective voices of the women on this list (straight wives) have crystallized the realization that I could have been a better husband/partner/friend to my wife. I feel like a complete life failure this A.M. as I face the possible loss of the most important person in my life. No do-overs, right? Feeling like I'm getting what I deserve.

* * *

I am currently still married to (and supporting) my wife, who can't decide whether she is bi or lesbian. I have lots of anger and lots of hurt. Don't really know where to start. Any advice?

* * *

My oldest daughter graduated from high school today. It was a very sad day. I couldn't shake it and hope that writing will help. The two things that make any event difficult these last years are my close relationship with my ex-wife's family and the loss of my two moms, my mother, and, most recently, my mother-in-law last summer. I'd talked with them every day, and they were my rocks through this whole awful experience. In sum, both I and my daughters lost the three most important women in our lives in the last three years. I'm all over the place being hit with loss upon loss. It started with my wife, then my mother and mother-in-law, and now my in-laws. "Why so much?"

I want to add, not subtract, from my life, but feel at a loss as to how to do that. Someone said to me yesterday that, when God closes a door, He opens a window. I may have said that myself as a poor attempt to make someone feel better about some unfortunate circumstance. I could use an open window because I need the fresh air. I can't seem to catch my breath between losses. Both my father-in-law and my sister-in-law found love again only months after death and divorce. It seems to me that God closed a door for them and decided to open a window straight away. It seems like doors are closing for me, and I see no windows.

Though I don't want to, I feel sorry for myself. Today should have been a happy day.

* * *

What does it mean if my husband says he's bi? From my experience, it will mean he will always be curious and will most likely "need" to act on that curiosity. I have found, through the experience of my own and others, that even the best marriages, even the most faithful, are susceptible. The sheer pull of same-sex attraction is stronger than desire, vows, will, and good intentions.

* * *

Allow me to foolishly and ignorantly hurt, get depressed, and cry. I feel like such a fool. While I wallowed in poverty, depression, sadness, and self-pity, the ex-wife and lesbian girlfriend built a nice nest for the future. I can't even hardly buy groceries. I can't pay the real estate taxes. I have almost nothing. My van is falling apart. While she affords a big beautiful home, I am hurting. I know I shouldn't, but it was a shock to see that home. Oops, house.

That (other) woman has ruined my life. DON"T YOU SAY SHE HASN'T. I HATE HER! I should have been more prepared. This life, as my dear friend says, it sucks. It is not fair. What did I do to find myself in this? Don't say it. I know we can reason ourselves out of these thoughts and feelings. But right now, I hurt.

Well, I wish I was joking and could call this a life. But, I can't. I will go walk the dog with my daughter. Maybe I will feel better. I just had to get this out.

* * *

I've been married for 16 years and have two beautiful daughters. Early April, my wife uttered those three words, "I am gay," and my world turned inside-out/upside-down. While I had suspected she was questioning her sexuality, I had no idea how far she had gone. The first couple of weeks were pretty much hell, but I recognized that this doesn't have to do with "me" and I'm working on looking after my kids and myself. She then did a big U-turn, saying she wanted us to stay together and didn't really understand any of it. She has been seeing a therapist (before and after) and, since coming out to me, has worked out that perhaps this has to do with some deeper issues from childhood. She has asked for some time to explore those before we do anything else. I'm happy to give her that time and, fundamentally, I want our relationship to stay together. (There are so many good things about it!) But, at the moment, I am feeling a bit in limbo and bit confused.

* * *

My husband and I have been married 37 years. We have four grown children. We haven't told them. I have known from about the beginning. I had no idea it would affect my life like it is right now. Once the kids moved out, he felt freer to see other men. At that point, we agreed to an open marriage. I don't know if I can really do it.

* * *

My wife and I had the best marriage, a 90% marriage: 90% of the time wonderful; 10%, it sucked. After disclosure, my wife says the marriage was between 60/40 or 50/50. The bad 50% was due to the sex issue and the other, issues that I acknowledge I need to fix (and I am). On 4/11, my wife came home about 4:30 AM from a party. She passed out, and her cell phone went off. I picked it up, and there was a message from her friend (now the girlfriend), saying she hoped she had gotten home OK and "Love you." This was a surprise. From there, I went digging back in the text messages and found more information and then lost it. Next was checking her email, when the full weight of what was going on hit me. So much talk about love and want and crap that I just was devastated. Later that day, I asked the GW (Gay wife) if she had seen the GF (girlfriend) the night before. She said, "No." This was the first time she had lied to me, and it was devastating. The next few days are a blur, filled with much crying and hurt and sitting at work incapacitated.

This changed on 4/16, when I talked with my sister-in-law, who said that my GW told her the night before that she thought she might be a lesbian. The lights just went off. There it was. All that crap with sex and intimacy that I had dealt with for the 5.5 years made sense. It was not me. No matter what I could do to change, to fix all the bad things, to create new things... nothing I could do would ever make me a woman. Not my fault. Looking back, this was a huge milestone.

* * *

My husband and I are newlyweds. We've been together longer. We have a 4-year-old son. I discovered my husband is bisexual. He is having affairs with other men, and he is abusive when I try to talk about it with him. I discovered gay porn on the computer and his own porn ads looking for men. I am devastated and confused. I don't know who to talk to. I can't tell my friends or family about it. I want to stay because we have a child. We've already separated once.

* * *

At 12:45 AM, I found the chat log: "I love you" followed by "I love you, too." And then "I wish we could cuddle" and "I'll sleep well on that note" were all I needed to get my blood boiling. It took me an hour of pacing and talking to her mom and my friend before I went upstairs and pulled her out of bed by her shirt. I took her down to the basement to confront her, and, filled with adrenaline, I asked, "What is it about this guy that is worth destroying out family and our marriage?"

"It's not a guy."

She'd been having an affair with a female for a couple weeks before I found out. Eight days later, she lost her job. My emotions went from massive depression to a fatherly/supportive role, as if she suddenly became my child. While she majorly screwed up, I had to be her rock.

I didn't like my new definition of "love" applied to someone who's supposed to be my wife and peer. She says she still loves me, but it doesn't carry the same weight it used to. Sometimes, I don't even return with my own, "I love you, too." After 16 years of being together, it seems so sudden, but it really shed light on our bedroom time we shared the past couple of years.

* * *

I'm so angry at all the wasted time I could scream. I was young and sexy and just wanted to be loved. Now I have to start all over at almost 60. I've been robbed!

* * *

About 6-12 months ago, I started feeling a growing distance from my wife. I didn't know what was going on and pressed her to tell me. Then on Earth Day, she showed me a picture of herself when she was a teenager with short hair and looking like a tomboy. I had seen it before and didn't understand what she was getting at, but then she said, "I am a lesbian." I was confused. We went to a pretty liberal college where the joke was that everyone was bisexual. I got angry and upset. I couldn't believe it or face it. I told her to get out of my sight, to get away from me and the kids.

That night I slept 2 hours. The following day, I went work and, after trying to maintain a normal face, broke down. I told my co-worker and my boss (a lesbian) and then couldn't take doing work, so went to be with friends. They supported me so much that I feel like, if I didn't have them... I wouldn't be here.

I am in therapy with my GW and on my own, working through what we will do. Divorce is looking like the most reasonable option. I'm not sure what we should tell the kids. It is so confusing, and I don't like being thrust in the closet with the GW. I also understand that she doesn't like it in there either. That's why she repressed all those feelings and married me.

* * *

My husband and I have been married for 24 years. We have 3 children. We own a business and work together. When I was pregnant with our first child, I came home and found my husband in bed with another man. Our marriage has never been good. When I look back on it, he's never been faithful.

Our eldest child asked me if Dad's gay. I denied it. They all suspect. We're filing for divorce.

* * *

My wife of 11 years (and partner of 16) told me last weekend that our marriage was over because she is "more queer" than she thought. Although I'd been tormenting myself with this suspicion for months, I'd convinced myself to trust her, thinking my suspicion was a product of my depression. So the reality came as a huge shock, and I'm having an incredibly difficult time accepting. It's only been a week, so this is quite raw. Yesterday (Halloween) is the anniversary of our first date and the day I asked her to marry me, so I'm a wreck.

I'm completely shattered, particularly by the deception. I can't accept she's leaving because she's gay. She insists it's not about "body parts," that she's attracted to a queer identity. That may be true, but, to me, it seems more cheap and cowardly. In my absence, she cheated on me and callously discarded 16 years of commitment, partnership, and friendship. Hiding behind a queer identity doesn't excuse not talking to me years ago when she sensed a problem in our relationship and certainly doesn't excuse months of lies more recently.

I was fighting depression before this news. My life is out of control now. I'm getting professional help (socialised medicine in the UK has faults, but I'm glad for it now!) Everyone says time helps, but I'm having a hard time making it to the next day, let alone next month.

* * *

I love this man with all my heart and have been with him for over half my life. I can't imagine life without him. I told him that I would give him 3 months to figure things out. He doesn't think he'll need that much time. In the meantime, my therapist has suggested couples therapy, which my husband has agreed to attend. I feel like I'm lying to everyone. I can't tell them what's going on. Anyone else been through something like this?

* * *

My husband and I have been married 7 years. We have young children. I found gay web surfing on the family computer. He said he wouldn't do it anymore. He said he wasn't attracted to men; he just enjoyed watching the sex. He lied. I found a stash of gay and bi porn movies in the closet.

* * *

My wife and I are pastors and long-time GLBT advocates. She has not had an affair or has a girlfriend waiting, but has come to a high level of certainty that she identifies sexually as a lesbian and does not see any sense in being in a sexless marriage. I don't see any either, but then I don't see much of "sense" in any of this. In my heart, I'm having a terrible time disengaging. It still feels good to be with her, to hold her, to care for her through the last couple of days when she's had the flu.

We talked more about separation this morning yet don't have a plan for telling the boys or our churches. I've talked with one colleague, a friend, and a lawyer. My biggest task is to disengage at some level, but I simply love her too much for that to be easy. The last two weeks have not torn us apart from each other, just torn me from my moorings. I'm not worried about my wife's honesty. We've been honest and open and loving. But I realize, at one level, that that's not enough anymore and it will be best for us to move on.

* * *

My husband and I have been married for 11 years. He finally told me he is gay. He told me has been trying to "come out" for years. He even showed me letters he'd written over the years that he saved. We have 2 girls. We're planning on staying together.

* * *

I suppose if I had the motivation to take a darker path, the reason is here. Luckily and through no particular effort on my part, it doesn't seem to appeal to me. Why my dentist gave me four refills of a narcotic painkiller for a minor procedure, I still question. I see people with a lot bigger problems than I have on a semi-regular basis and realize that, while TGT is unlucky, unfortunate, whatever life could be for 95% of the world's population actually is worse. Large tragedies occur every day for no apparent reason, and a motto I've created for myself is "There are a lot of screwed up people in the world, and, honestly, I'm not one of them." I try not to give myself too many excuses. Of course, the real issue is that in my heart of hearts, I'm just not ready to let her go.

* * *

My husband and I have been married 13 years. He told me he was in love with a man. He also told me he is bi-sexual and has been going to motels, meeting up with other men, and having sex. I asked him to leave. A week later, he called and said he had made a mistake and wanted to come home. I said, "Yes." I still love him. He says he wants our relationship/family to work, and so do I. We have agreed to counseling. I don't think this will ever go away.

* * *

Over Thanksgiving, she told me she wanted to leave and had found someone else. I was very upset. She told the children the next day. This has devastated me, my children, and our families because she feels it is OK to bring her girlfriend around our children. She's been doing it regularly and lying to me about it. Two of my children are from my marriage, and the third is from my soon-to-be-ex-wife's first. When the divorce is final, they'll all stay with me and see their mother when her work schedule permits. Since I never formally adopted my oldest, she can take him out of the house at any time. I am terrified at that possibility. My son is a great kid, and I don't want to see him hurt any more.

* * *

My husband and I have been married 4 years. We've been together 10. We have a 6 year old daughter. I always felt there was something wrong. He was never really happy. He admitted to me this week he is bisexual and has always known. I am trying to sort out all of my very mixed emotions. I don't know if he can be faithful to us.

* * *

My husband and I have been married 33 years. We have 5 children. My husband received a text from a man asking him for sex. When he realized I knew, he erased all his messages and lied about it.

* * *

My husband and I have been married 19 years. We have two children. Last year, my husband told me, "I think I might be gay." We talked. We want to stay together and make it work. We are agreeing to an open marriage so he can find himself. It's very hard. Of all things that could affect a marriage, I never suspected this. My children do not know. We aren't telling them.

* * *

My husband of 29 years filed for divorce. We have three children. He's been unfaithful most of the marriage, surfing same-sex sites, excusing it away by telling me I don't give him enough attention. He's been having "three ways" in bathrooms and lying about it. I'm angry and will be glad when all of this is over.

* * *

I've been married for 12 years. It's always been hard, but now my wife says she is gay. I don't know how to handle that. I know it's not about me, but the kids and I don't understand. I have thought about bringing her girlfriend into our marriage – maybe which would help. I play it off like it don't bother me, but it does. I just want my family to stay together. Is that wrong, or should I just divorce and move?

About six months ago, my wife seemed a bit depressed, so I made a concerted effort to help keep the house clean, do some vacuuming, give her an extra hug here and there, bring home flowers to help brighten up the house, etc. One night, lying in bed, she asked why I was being so nice and doing all these "extra" things. I told her I thought she needed some extra love and I was making a concerted effort to help her out and make her life a little easier. She started crying. I was completely blown away. Here I was, trying to make her happier, and now she's bawling her eyes out. She said that this behavior was very "unlike" me (which wasn't true). It was totally bizarre. Now, looking back, it was her being crushed with guilt over (1) her affair and (2) the fact she was gay and hadn't told me yet.

More of this stuff pops into my head almost every day, where I think, "Ahh, that's what was going on. Now it makes sense." I still can't believe I didn't realize she was having an affair (with a woman who's a close family "friend"). I thought I was more attentive than to let something like that slip by. I guess maybe sometimes you don't see what you don't want to see.

* * *

My fiancé and I have lived together for almost a year. When I was pregnant, I discovered an email to him from a guy who said he couldn't wait to have sex with him! I could hardly breathe. When I asked him about it, he came out. He's been living a gay lifestyle since, and I'm alone. We have an infant daughter. I stay because he takes care of me financially.

* * *

I'm new – didn't think I'd ever be in this situation. My wife told me two months ago she was a lesbian, after 16 years of marriage. We have no children, but I love her very much. Though she says she still loves me and I think it's true, I'm feeling abandoned and angry whenever I hear anything about her lesbian life. I thought I could handle it at least until we decided what to do. It's getting rougher, as I realize she plans to be out most every night. We haven't told friends or family. I thought that was a good idea because it would protect her a bit and not make more problems than we can handle. However, that leaves me with no one to talk things through with. Lately, I've taken to just avoiding her, so as not run into the barbs.

* * *

My husband and I have been married 7 years. We have two very young children. Our marriage has never been good. Most recently, I found gay porn while surfing on the computer. He has excused away what I know were male hook-ups, subscriptions to gay magazines, texting, and emails. I'm preparing for divorce.

* * *

I am heartbroken. My wife's mental health knowledge gives her the edge enough to not get the help she needs. Her family is enabling her behavior by giving her unconditional support, not valuing the marriage and despising me because she's telling a significantly different story. The hard part is that I wish there was some way to put this back together. I love her. She was my wife. We were married, not just dating or in love. There were signs of trouble, but many are common for the first couple of years of marriage. It seems they exploded once she had that freedom living separately from me (for what was supposed to only be 2½ months). Although this sounds like a "Jerry Springer-ish" story, we were pretty Christian. She worked as a counselor in Catholic schools, attended services weekly, and served food at the homeless shelter. We taught Sunday school together.

I didn't want a divorce – the biggest possible failure in my life. I took her "in sickness and in health" and wanted to work through this. I have a hard time believing she is this way. I accept it is a possibility, but also can't rule out what her working at such a horrible place (prison) could have done to her – also our being apart and her troubled upbringing. Believing our marriage was real, I feel cheated. I miss that love of a marriage. A Catholic annulment doesn't seem right. Loving someone else feels very wrong.

The most frustrating part is that I am keeping her secret. I want the whole world to know and don't like being the scapegoat for her cover up. Yet I feel that if I call her licensing board, it will force her to retaliate. She has already called my job to bad mouth me. I haven't slept in six months. I know it has to get better, because I can't keep living like this. I'm hoping the pain will eventually subside. It already isn't as sharp, but still painful nonetheless.

* * *

I was married to my husband for 10 years. I divorced when our son was 3. I discovered my now ex-husband gay web surfing in our third year of marriage. By year 5, he was actively seeking gay married men, texting, hooking up for sex, and advertising himself on gay sites, wanting sex and companionship. He's in the closet. He's never admitted to being gay.

* * *

For almost a month, my wife hasn't had contact with the GF (girl friend). Things are ok. I know this is not what I want in a marriage, but I don't want to give up yet. With three small boys, I'm stuck with her no matter what. We are going through with the separation but have not divided assets, something I'm sure will cause a fight. I know she feels entitled to everything, including custody, alimony. But, if she wants to make it easy, it's going to be my way. I will not support her new lifestyle if that's what she wants to do.

There's still a chance we will stay together. It is up to her. I'm at the end of my rope and cannot take one more act of cheating. We get along wonderfully, and, if I didn't think we could still have some sort of marriage, I would walk away. I don't think she realizes the pain she's put me through. I'm still with her because of our children. I can't imagine not being with them every single day and will put up with a lot to continue to have that. But I cannot be lied to and cheated on anymore. It almost makes the gay thing insignificant for a time. I know we will have to deal with it at some point.

I'm leaving my options open. One thing I know. I was at a party last week, and there were some super-hot single women, probably 10 years younger than me. I was like a deer in the headlights. I don't even know how to talk to women anymore.

* * *

I'm not married yet. My fiancé says he isn't gay nor bisexual. He says he has an insatiable curiosity of men. I have to get out of this relationship without compromising who I am. It's a nightmare, and I can't wake up.

* * *

I've been married 19 years. I'm struggling. We're a Christian family. I discovered my husband's obsession when we got our computer back after repairs. When I booted it up, there was a gay male site on the log-in screen. When I confronted him, he denied. I dug deeper and found proof of his activity on the sites. He came clean. He's had more than ten lovers. I can't stay married. I know my husband is gay and cheating. He's not out. We have a daughter. She won't know.

* * *

I've been married 16 years. We have adult children. This year, my husband decided he was gay and was openly seeking relationships with gay men. It's been over a year since we've had sex. I've filed for divorce.

* * *

I am a 60 year old married woman. We have no children. My husband visits men's toilets and meets men for sex. I became aware of this last year. I haven't decided whether or not to file for divorce.

* * *

I'm not married yet. My fiancé told me he had m2m sex with a friend when he was in college. He says, since then, he's never been with another man. He likes to fantasize about sex with a man and look at gay porn. He calls himself "bi-or bi-curious" but says he doesn't have any emotional interest in men. He says it's all about the sex. I don't know if I can live with this. He tells me he wants to be monogamous.

* * *

I've suspected my wife might be gay for a long time. Since she came out, it's been an emotional roller coaster. I'm 44, married for 17 years. We have two amazing daughters, 11 and 13, and I want to minimize any pain to them. Though weird, right away I felt optimistic without knowing exactly why. For one thing, I started noticing more attractive women. At the same time, I felt closer to my wife, less resentment than I did before I knew the truth. I see her really struggling for the first time ever, and I want to help her. Unfortunately, she's not looking for help. Of course, the downside of feeling optimistic is that each time she pulls back to denial or tries to shrug this all off, it hurts me more. But I know we've made some progress. I started seeing a therapist for the first time.

* * *

I found out after a strange night out, where we both did some things with this girl that I wish I wouldn't have. I'm not an innocent man but had never touched another woman (since I'd been with my wife). I was horror-stricken with guilt, but then my wife tells me that she wants to be with her again (alone). She confesses she's been fighting these feelings for a long time and wants to have ongoing relationships with other women.

Strangely, I'm fond of her girlfriend, and we have been able to keep our friendship alive. (I am confused about that as well.) I've been fighting emotional highs and lows these three weeks. My wife and I have better sex than we've had for many years, and she's very kind to me most of the time.

Some of the issues I struggle with every day are:

(1) If she's going to date other women, where does that leave me? My heart tells me to be true to myself and remain loyal, but the thought pisses me off;

(2) She doesn't want her son to find out. I am a step-dad; he is 16. Why should I bear that burden of lying to him? What am I going to tell him when his mother is out all night?

(3) She adamantly does not want to divorce, and I truly love her. But, I'm not sure I have the fortitude to stick around if she wants to date other people; and

(4) (This one really gets me.) She says that sex with a woman is not a violation of our marriage, but me having sex with another woman would be. Screw that!!! Are gay people not feeling intimate emotions and bonding when they have sex? I thought that was what this was all about.

* * *

I have been married 20 years. I caught my husband surfing gay porn nearly eight years ago. He won't talk about it. He shuts me out of everything. Our sex life has been nil for the last 15 years. We have two teenage children.

* * *

It's only been a month since she told me, but we've had a lot of conversations. I try to give her space and time to herself as often as possible because I can see the stress it is having on her health and psyche. It was a bombshell for me, but I'm a survivor. I know I'll get through it. I don't have to like it, but I do have to deal with it, and we have to make the transition as easy on our kids as possible.

I'm trying to be as mature and supportive as I can be, and she's trying to do the same for me. We're best friends on this road together. We're being as up front and honest with one another as we can... which isn't always easy for either of us. Sometimes she doesn't want to talk about it or tell me everything because she thinks it will hurt me, but I told her it would hurt me more if she lied. I know that, when I voice my anger and anguish over some things, she gets hurt, but she tells me she needs to know what I'm thinking and feeling. It was tough last night because she asked me what I wanted for my birthday and I told her I wanted to make love to her one more time before we finally separate.

The road ahead isn't easy. As long as we're on it together, we can get through it and make her coming out, our split, and divorce as amicable as possible. We're going to lose friends and even family members, and they're not going to understand it. They don't have to understand, but they will have to accept that this is the way things are going to be, if they want to be a part of our lives.

* * *

I've been married 22 years. We have a teenage son. I discovered that my husband had a sexual relationship with another married man for eight years. Once caught, my husband finally admitted he was gay. His boyfriend separated from his wife. My husband moved out to live with him. He wants to remain permanently separated. I remain on his insurance, and I have other assets. He does not want a divorce. A year later, my son asked him to come home. My husband and I talked, and he moved back in. It's painfully clear he's in love with this man and needs him in his life.

* * *

I've been married ten years. I have two young children. I caught my husband looking at gay porn magazines. He said he was just curious. Since that time, he's been texting and emailing men. We've been through counseling. It's no use. He's not honest. We can't decide if we're going to separate or divorce.

* * *

The past seven days have been some of the worst of my life. Many of you have read my post about my soon-to-be-ex-wife's violent outburst and our custody disagreements. Each time I think I have made it far enough that I am turning the corner or see the light at the end of the tunnel, I discover that I really have miles and miles to go.

I've learned only two things I'm fully sure of. The first is that TGT (the gay thing) messes up everything. You discover you were headed down a blind alleyway and have to go back again and make course corrections. At what point do we finally emerge healthy enough that we can regain our confidence in ourselves to trust our own judgment? I suppose it's different for each of us. The second thing I know for sure is that the Str8s support group is comprised with some of the finest people I've even known. Your support, understanding, and patience are unparalleled. You have gotten me through the dark days and continue to help. Even when the pain is my own to endure, your example hardens my determination to rise about TGT and my own mistakes, to survive this, and eventually emerge at the end as the person I want to be.

* * *

After 20 years of marriage, my husband told me he's gay. He says he loves me and wants to stay married. He says he wants to go to counseling. We have two teenage children. We do have sex, and it's still good. I have no reason to believe he's been cheating. I'm lost and don't know what to do.

* * *

I've been married 3 years and think my husband is gay. We have a 6-month- old. I've always felt something was wrong. He never touches me. He never initiates sex. He never kisses me.

We are never intimate. During my pregnancy, he wouldn't have sex with me at all. He never showed affection. He excused it away by saying he was nervous about becoming a father. After the baby was born, it got worse. He rejected me all the time. I was suspicious and started snooping. I found Viagra in his coat pocket and questioned him. He denies having it. I found the cell phone bill and saw the same three numbers called frequently. Men answered. His phone is always locked and so is his computer. It's a nightmare.

* * *

I've been married ten years. I feel alone. I discovered my husband has been having sex with men for most of our married life. We never did have chemistry. We never really had a bond. He's deep in the closet and won't come out. Knowing I want a divorce, he's seeking to openly date a woman. He's on gay sites daily. I can't wait to get out of hell. I'll never have closure.

* * *

I have been married 18 years. I have 6 children. My husband told me about one encounter he had in college long before we ever were married. Since our vows, I have found gay porn magazines and gay website activity. He always kept me at home with the children while he traveled. He got sick, went to the doctor, and they thought he had cancer. He's HIV+. I'm not sick; I've been tested repeatedly. Now that all the lies are gone and honest communication is in our lives, we're trying to work through this to stay married.

* * *

I've been married 42 years. We have two adult children. I'm 63. My husband has not wanted sex with me for years. I found he'd been visiting gay porn sites and looking for male companions on adult “friend finders.” We are both very deeply involved in our church. I'm filing for divorce. Our children do not know about their father. They'd be devastated.

* * *

I’m in my second marriage. I’m 55. We have been married 7 years. I am his third wife. We are a blended family with 2 of my own and 3 of his. They are all adults. I discovered a gay website recently. He didn’t sign out. He says he’s been curious. He says he loves me and wants to stay married. I’m a Christian, and I’m battling with my beliefs about homosexuality.

* * *

I've been married 3 months. My husband told me he was bisexual before we got married. I have a 5 year old son from my first marriage. We agreed to monogamy, but I don't think I'm enough for him. I think he needs more. There's no intimacy to sex, and there are certain things he won't do. He shuts down when I tell him what I like or need in the bedroom. I don't know what to do. I feel like he fantasizes about men when he's with me.

* * *

I've been married 17 years. We have three teenage daughters. My husband told me just weeks before we got married that he was interested in men. I wanted to cancel the wedding and didn't. Our marriage has always been a struggle, but he's always been a wonderful provider and given our daughters a wonderful life. I feel like I've never ever been enough.

* * *

I have been married 29 years! He was my first and only sexual experience, and it's always been miserable. I've caught him on gay sites, and he says I've driven him to do it. He says it's all me. He says I'm frigid. He says I pushed him away. There can't be anything further from the truth. We have two adolescent boys. He says I trapped him. He's verbally and emotionally abusive. He tells me he wasted his life with me. He's had STD's in the past. I don't have a job and cannot support myself to divorce him.

* * *

My husband is in the military. I have been married for 4 years. I found letters and pictures of a man he's been sleeping with in a lock box in our bedroom. I told him to leave. He did. He was deployed to war, and he begged me to get back together. I'm torn. Our daughter is 3, and I hate to take her daddy away from her; but I can't go on with this, knowing my husband is in love with another man.

* * *

I have been married for 33 years. We have an adult daughter. I am Christian and am struggling. I have strong religious beliefs about "gay," and yet I love my husband. I found out just after being married that my husband had homosexual tendencies. I found out more recently that my husband liked showing naked pictures of himself to other men. He told me he was seeing a therapist, only to find out he never went and was using the time slot to seek sex with men. We didn't divorce; however, we did separate for almost two years. He wanted to come back home and did. The next two decades were not easy, but he was devoted to us. Our son found porn on the computer and confronted his father. Our son also told people in our church, and that led to banning my husband from many of the church activities. He's had suicidal thoughts and has said he's never been attracted to women, only men.

* * *

I'm divorcing my husband of 22 years. We have two boys. Not 3 years into our marriage, my husband told me he is curious about men but he's not gay. We stayed married, bought a house, and had our children. I've always had my doubts. Years ago, I received an anonymous letter telling me to get tested for HIV. There were pictures of my husband enclosed with the letter. The author of the letter admitted to having a long term relationship with my husband. He'd found lumps on his body and thought he had cancer. Turns out he's sick. He has HIV. To this day, my husband denies he's gay. He calls himself "bi-attracted." He's angry I've filed.

* * *

I have been married 7 years. I'm divorcing. We do not have any children. I found graphic emails to other men our first year together. He was very angry when I confronted him, and he brushed it off as curious. Most recently, he's been advertising for men and women on Craig's List and, when I confronted him, he hit me. I can't stay.

* * *

I've been married 32 years. We've been together nearly 40. Almost a year ago, I discovered my husband has been having an affair with another man. I found out because the man he was seeing called me to tell me my husband was cheating on him. We have an adult daughter. We're in counseling. I'm 73, and I have no idea how to start my life over.

* * *

I've been married for 30 years. My husband came out to me on our 10th anniversary. No one else knows. I've been in his closet. He has a companion. I've never looked at another man. I don't know how much longer I can do this.

* * *

I have been married 11 years. We have 3 children. My husband recently told me he wants to know what it's like to have oral sex with another man. Over the years, we've been fighting about his need for gay porn and gay website surfing. He tried to hide the folder on our computer, and I found it. He's angry. He doesn't feel like he should have to choose between his need for a man and his family. He wants both. I just need and want out of this marriage. I discovered he's advertised himself on Craig's List, looking for men. I also discovered he goes to adult book stores and goes into booths to have sex with men. I'm exhausted.

* * *

"First cries" like these sound out in those desperate first moments of darkness, where everything in our lives is unrecognizable and we're too numb to do anything but cry out and weep in silence.

We're often asked, "After all that pain and numbness, how did you cope?" Our answer is simple. The journey is not. We each had to forge through the fire.

Chapter 4
Forging Through the Fire

The melting point of steel is about 2800 degrees Fahrenheit. Here's a fact about one method of forging this metal: Due to the exposure of the extreme heat, the metal actually restructures internally and comes out stronger. Sound familiar?

Annabelle…

Six weeks after moving to Russia, my husband of 26 years disclosed to me that he's gay. I'm 41. The only reason he told me was because he thought he'd contracted an STD. The next 48 hours, I knew I needed to talk to someone.

I Skyped friends in Arizona. I also found, by luck, an English-speaking counselor in Moscow and saw her to get through the initial shock. My mother, whom I wouldn't have told anyway, had passed just three months after we moved to Russia. I have 3 sisters, and, with the dynamic we have, I'm not sure I could trust telling them without being mocked. His sister, who is a wonderful friend to me, is someone I found I could talk to.

I also did web searches for support for my new straight spouse identity, and I actually found the Straight Spouse Network. It's an international support group for men and women whose spouse is gay, bisexual, transgender, or lesbian. It has helped me connect with other woman in my shoes.

When he first told me, I remember yelling at him, "You took me away from my support system and now who can I talk to? Why didn't you tell me this when you realized it ten years ago? Was it something I lacked? Did you not trust me?"

When I look back on last year, I think my husband was at a breaking point. As he was confessing, a weight much larger than I realized was lifting from his shoulders. Evidently, he had been hanging on to this for years. Even if this STD issue had not come up, I don't think it would have taken much more time before he came out. We have two kids, 11 and 14. They don't know. My husband and I feel that ours is an intimate marriage issue, not a family issue. We are planning to stay married and are working through the dynamics of embracing "gay."

Initially, I told him I wanted monogamy. When I realized he would stay true to that commitment, I decided I needed to be fair and offered the thought of us having an open marriage so he could have a companion, with the stipulation that I always come first. I told him if that priority ever changes, then his relationship with his boyfriend must stop. He's agreed. We are intimate and have a great relationship. We work through our issues day to day. He's a man of character. I guess I demanded monogamy at first because I felt like, if I agreed to have an open marriage, I'd be giving him away. Now I feel like it's just the opposite. By allowing him the freedom to embrace his need for a man, I've deepened our relationship and I have a stronger marriage than I did before. It helped us to grow. We were talking one night and he asked me, "If I told you at 23 when we had two small kids, would you have stayed?"

I said I don't know, but here we are now. It's not about coulda, shoulda, woulda; it's about right here, right now. We met in college our sophomore year and have been together since. We lived in Texas and, about 9 years later, moved to Arizona. Now we're in Russia. This is our first overseas assignment.

When I look back on it, there were things leading up to his coming out. One of the eye openers over the last couple of years was that he always erased the history on the family computer, making excuses that the computer needed to run faster. He did everything wrong for the two years leading up to his coming out and has done everything right since. Upon disclosure, he called and told his parents and told them to place money in an account so that I could get on a plane with the kids and leave.

When he was disclosing, he said, "I expect you to go. I don't want you to, but I've accepted that you would. Half of what I have is yours. You never have to worry." He didn't try to persuade me from thinking about anything. "I want to work on this but understand if you don't." He never made excuses.

When I'd have days where I'd be mad or upset, he'd never question it. He'd be supportive. He never said, "Just get over it." He never was mad that I was mad. He's always allowed me to work through all my emotions. Once he was finally honest, he's been consistently honest. I think it was a huge relief, and he feels he's been very lucky to keep his family through all this.

Being that my husband does have a desire to date men, we do have new rules. We talked about the fact he can have a buddy. The buddy cannot live here. For many reasons, that would be impossible and unacceptable. When we go back home to Arizona, he has a gay married friend. His friend isn't out. I think his wife knows, not sure. I have met his married friend. I have a bit of guilt about the fact his friend's wife may not know. It's not a gay issue; it is an issue of right or wrong. I struggle with it.

I've been asked if I want a boyfriend. No. My needs are met emotionally and physically. I don't feel the need to escape. There are no eggshells. I'm in my own skin. In the beginning, I had a lot of questions. It was painful for him, but he answered all my questions openly, and, now, it's no big deal. He is a person of character. He did make a huge mistake. But, when he said he was coming clean, he did so and took full responsibility.

I even went with him when he did get tested. I told him, "I want to hear what you tell the doctors. I want to know what you tell them."

He told the doctors, "I need to make sure for my wife that she is taken care of and protected."

The doctors even took a swab and put it up his urethra, and -- I can't lie – that part of me did feel a bit good about the pain he felt.

We have an open relationship, and his companion has a yearning to have the same dynamic with his wife as my husband and me. My husband and I are intimate. I have no desire to look for someone. For right here, right now, it's good. If that ever changes, then the rules are that we have an open marriage. If ever I get uncomfortable or I feel his priorities have changed, then it's he who must end his relationship and focus on his marriage. His analogy and explanation about having an open marriage is "This is not instead of you… it's in addition to you." So I've expressed to him openly, if that priority ever changes, it's over. I have accepted the risk. Staying married to him means that eventually he may come out as gay. He has promised to be honest about this. I love the life we have formed since disclosure and trust that he will be forthcoming. His male friend is not in the same country. Right now, it's more like a support for him, and he benefits from this.

I think the key is real communication. Communication with my husband is better than ever. I told him I don't care how much it hurts, you have to tell me everything. Our relationship has improved. This honesty has spread into other areas of our marriage. We talk about everything. Nothing is out of range. It changed our dynamics. So, it's not that I'm happy about gay, but it's had a positive impact on who we are and how we live together. We've kept it between us. No one in my family knows. His family knows and those I've told.

We work from a place of honesty. If he is missing the "bi" side, he tells me. I have told him I accept this side and would rather know than not know. This is where we base every conversation: on honesty first, even if it hurts. It's the dynamics. It's the communication and the honesty. We can tell each other everything no matter how painful. Everything is on the table. It has to be. I know I run the risk of him realizing that he is gay, not bi. I willingly take that risk because he had been so honest.

I tell him that I will be the ex-wife at his gay wedding if that is what this eventually becomes.

If I could offer any advice to a closeted husband or wife, it would be to be honest no matter how painful. Don't let fear keep you from honesty. Don't make assumptions that your wife or husband won't want to make it work. Just come out. You can redefine your marriage, but you can't redefine it if you don't know what you have to work with. You both have to know your priorities, and you both have to be 100% committed to marriage. You can't want part of it or some of it; you have to want all of it, and both of you must have the same definition and stick to it whatever the new definition is for your marriage. Some people can't get past the label. It's different for everyone. I said to my husband a long time ago, "We're not the couple we were 20 years ago, and we're not the couple we were 10 years ago." Right here, right now, it works. It's a very different marriage, and our needs are met. It can't be one-sided. I've found I can handle situations I never have dreamed I could! I am ok with this because I am growing every day as a human being in the way I handle this marriage.

What kind of support does my husband have? My husband is on a men's only site. It's been a terrific source of comfort for him.

He came across a great analogy to explain an open marriage. "Sometimes you want steak, and sometimes you want chocolate."

I told him, "I hope that you want steak because that's the main course."

He said, "Of course!"

We talked about the fact that if it ever changed, so will the rules of our marriage. I have been very open about the need to know. He recently expressed an interest in gay saunas. My response, "Keep me in the know."

I know he needs to express this side of himself, but it has to be with my knowledge and consent as well as our health and well-being.

Here we are. We're married 26 years, have two children, and we're living in Russia. Am I happy? Yes. More importantly, am I content? Yes. Most importantly, are my needs met and is my marriage vibrant and strong? Yes. Here's an original quote that sums it up well. After a therapy session, my husband and I went out to dinner, where he made a toast, "...to the best 'us' that comes out of this!" I know he means "us" as individuals as well as a couple – whatever may come of "us."

Travis...

In 2001, I married my high school sweetheart. (We were both 23.) We had been dating for almost six years, even surviving a long-distance relationship during college. This was my second actual relationship. I hadn't been confident with girls as a teen and so thought I was finally getting into something good and would make a go of it. For a few years, we were traveling every year or two between each other's career-oriented jobs and daydreaming what life would be like once we settled down to start a family. In 2004, we moved to Connecticut for her to start a summer job. As time wore on, my wife became emotionally distant, particularly in showing public affection and romantic interest in the bedroom. It felt like I was sleeping next to a cold, damp log. When she DID try to get romantic, it seemed forced, and I felt like I was taking advantage of her — not a turn-on in my opinion.

This continued for a year, when she got accepted to grad school, twelve hours away by car. Four months after our move nearer her school, guess who came to visit over New Year's?!? During those few days, I picked up on enough vibes to tell something was amiss. In a moment of clarity, I realized, "Holy shit! She's falling for this other woman! She can't even talk to me about French kissing, and here she's basically attaching herself emotionally to this girlfriend?"

I distanced myself from her for a few days after the visit to see if she noticed any change. When she picked up on how cold-shouldered I was behaving, I confronted her. She admitted having romantic feelings towards this woman but thought it was just because they had a good friendship. She started a dialog among the three of us, and everything seemed to smooth out.

Meanwhile, my wife would occasionally ask in the dead of night if I was happy or wished I'd married someone else. She knows about my affection for women now that I'm more confident, and I told her of the almost-girlfriend I had in college even though nothing happened: just a single parting kiss once I made up my mind to stay with my now wife.

Now that I'd figured out her deviations, our talks became deeper. I know when it's coming: a fog rises between us for a couple days, both getting emotionally distant until I give in and ask what she's thinking or she says those four words that never precede good news: "We need to talk." Figuring out what to say and how to say it in these circumstances is difficult, as if I don't know how I feel. Instead, I get despondent, and it looks like I've given up on the relationship.

Bottom line, I've taken enough time to observe the situation from a distance and found that I'm not in love with her any more -- not due to her newly questioning orientation but something larger: the spark in our relationship went out. I've seen more of what the world has to offer in terms of other partners, and I'm not satisfied anymore. Also, I've become more adventurous in outdoor activities, while she's remained cautious and inhibited by these outlets. Compounding things farther, she had difficulties finishing her master's degree. Her lack of success in this and our relationship led to numerous crying fits and drained me of any compassion towards her.

Coincidentally, we both did private research before the shit hit the fan and chalked up our "sparklessness" as the "typical" seven-year marriage slump. After she came out with her feelings, we began seeing a counselor. My wife tried to pin my reluctance to salvage our relationship on embedded grief due to my father's death when I was 12! I attributed to that experience the strength, sensitivity, and maturity I demonstrate today. I am accepting, too, of a number of close friends' being gay/lesbian, so it's not a homophobia driving my feelings.

I believed her when she said she hasn't been sexual with or kissed another woman yet, and she won't know if this is real until she tries it. So we agreed to separate for the summer. I'd take a better job out of town; she could stay and have the space she needs to explore these urges. I could do the same, and we could see where that takes us. Soon after agreeing on a trial separation, though, she decided she still wanted me and wanted to know that we were okay. I was beyond shock but had a hard time finding words or feelings to respond. How did the spotlight suddenly turn on ME?!? I thought SHE had the problem! DID I want to stay in the relationship? Needless to say, she called often and visited frequently on weekends…not exactly conducive to testing other relationships. I was easily angered coping with the situation, so I released a LOT of tension through physical exertion: brutal exercises, long runs, bike rides, hard paddles in a canoe around the lake.

Wondering if moving to a new location for a fresh start would help anything, she accepted a permanent position on the east coast. We moved but fell into the same patterns: me resenting being the unacknowledged homemaker and source of extra earnings, while she stays at work for most of the waking day. My attraction to her and her personality crashed, which led us to a longer string of counseling sessions (most as couples, some individually) that helped me more than I thought they would. I began to realize that my lack of emotion throughout this directly related to the loss of my love for my wife when all this started, a Pavlovian Response, it's called, to her Platonic Affair. Another prime factor is the reason we married soon after college: a casual observation my mom made. I hadn't thought through it long enough to realize that maybe one or both of us had changed significantly during those four years spent frequently apart, me, maturing, and she, holding onto those little girl daydreams.

None of this came up before because I didn't want to hurt her or have her family and our friends resent me. Instead, I let my OWN resentment build until it was too late, being finally released by her swaying emotions. These words and feelings came from me, not the counselor; I just didn't have the guts to admit to them before. Now I'm told that the only truth is how I feel, not how others may or may not feel about me.

I'm not saying I lacked commitment – far from it. I was still monogamous, supported her financially and emotionally though three years of graduate school, and did the finances and most of the household tasks. I've recently identified that all was done out of FAMILIAL love, not SENSUAL love. I treated the tasks as should's and ought-to's instead of a desire to do it FOR HER. Not healthy. Living together turned into an unfortunate housemate situation instead of one based on mutual love and understanding.

Last spring, I got tired of picking up her slack, and my irritation got out of control. We agreed to a true separation, but she wanted regular contact to see how things were going. I felt I'd be happier with little contact because close proximity and the issues blinded me to why I fell in love with her – her personality and our common interests and ideals. The only chance to find how I honestly felt about her was to be on my own and assess what, if anything was missing.

Keeping an open mind, I realized that nothing was missing. I gained freedom, health, confidence, and enjoyment in my activities, and, if not happiness, then at least a greater sense of fulfillment. As my wife and I tried to do things we both liked, it still felt incomplete and forced. The underlying drive to be together, the love, was missing. If we were to meet anew tomorrow, I'm pretty sure I wouldn't feel anything for her beyond a casual friendship. So, after over five months on my own, it's over. Fortunately, we don't have any kids. I still love her, but in a strictly familial way that would exist even after we divorce. It's nice to be able to come to terms with my decision, knowing it's the right one to make.

"What would you say if the she was a he?"...

I met Paul when I was a sophomore in college. He was handsome, smart, and hilarious. As students, we were members of the freshman orientation staff. Our friendship developed over the semester we trained for our summer job. Before long, we were best friends and spent hours talking on the phone and in person. This friendship led to a dating relationship. Everything seemed to be going along fine until I found out I was pregnant. Three months later, we married and thus began my seventeen year odyssey.

The early years were tough. We lived in married housing while Paul finished school. Our daughter was born soon after. We moved far from home for his job, and he hated the city and his work from the beginning of our relocation. After six stressful months, we went back to school for me to finish my bachelor's degree and for him to get his master's degree. After we both graduated, he got his first real job and seemed to be very happy. But, after less than a year, he was already restless and ready to find a new job. He had issues with his boss, co-workers, the church, and the town. We ended up staying for four miserable years.

Then, out of the blue, opportunity came knocking: his ex-boss had a position for him out of state, far from our families. Before considering this move, we made a trip out west to check out the city and job situation. The town seemed like a dream right out of the 50's. Everyone had a beautiful home, and the schools were great for our daughter. We were sold. We bought a beautiful home, and I began my starring role of Donna Reed reincarnated. We had the perfect home, lovely neighbors, a friendly church; he had the perfect job; and our daughter went to the perfect school. Somewhere between years one and two, something went wrong. There was a rift between us and our Sunday school class; I never could figure out what happened. Shortly thereafter, his boss suddenly lost his job, and it wasn't long before Paul's job was on the chopping block. Again, I never knew what was going on behind the scenes and probably never will. After only two beautiful years of our "perfect" life, we were making plans to move back home to Florida. He had no job and no prospects, but we were going "home." He finally got a lead on a job, and we were back in business. He felt settled in a job.

Over time, he became more obsessed with our little family being perfect in every way. I had to be thin and keep a perfect home, and our daughter had to make perfect grades and excel in all activities. The stress was palatable. As the tension built, he began showing signs of depression and anxiety. He'd say, "Help me!" but wouldn't explain what he meant. I had no idea what was causing this internal angst. Lack of exercise, poor eating habits, and long hours at work led him to a near heart attack. By the time he agreed to go to the doctor, he had developed high blood pressure, high cholesterol, and was forty pounds overweight. The doctor said he had to change his lifestyle, start on medication, and deal with his depression. He sent him to a psychiatrist.

This experience seemed to change him. He began exercising regularly, eating right, and taking care of himself. Within a few months, he was looking great and feeling better. But the long hours at work continued. At times, I had difficulty getting in touch with him by phone. This was very unusual.

Before this time, he was a total family man, and now he was distracted. One evening, he had not come home by 11:30 pm, and I became distraught. I called his cell phone over twenty times without an answer. Finally he answered, and I confronted him. I asked him where he was and who he was with; eventually he broke down and told me he was seeing a woman at his office, which was a total fabrication. He cried as he told me how sorry he was for hurting me. I was stunned. How could this man who I loved, trusted, and was totally devoted to be cheating on me? I spent the next month trying to get him to explain why he was doing this to us. I was going out of my mind.

One evening when we were taking our evening walk, he told me he was planning to go on a cruise Mother's Day weekend. My reaction was "How can you do this to me, and on Mother's Day?" to which he responded, "*What would you say if the she was a he?"*

These words swirled around in my brain. My mind could not process what my ears were hearing. What did this mean? When it finally hit me, I started screaming and crying, nearly collapsing on the ground. My head was spinning, and I couldn't catch my breath. What was happening to me? All I kept thinking was "My life as I know it is over."

His reaction to my hysteria was "If I'd known you were going to get this upset, I wouldn't have told you." He actually believed the truth would make me feel better.

I was in a state of shock. What was I going to do? I couldn't tell anybody. They would think I was crazy or judge me. I didn't even tell my parents. Every day was painful, and I tried in vain to hide my sorrow from our daughter. I couldn't eat, sleep, or concentrate. The tears were constantly flowing. It seemed that, once he had admitted his secret, it was okay for him to stay out all night. Every evening, he didn't come home. I'd stay up all night and wait for the sun to come up in the morning so I could go to work and not think about what was really going on in my life. Thank God for work; it was a distraction. For weeks, I moved slowly through a total fog; I lost weight, was short of breath, had headaches and chest pain. My boss finally told me, "If you don't get some help, you're going to have a stroke." She could have never imagined what torment I was going through. I finally had to take action and get a hold of my life. As a social worker, I knew I needed to get help.

I went to the library and tried to find a book that mentioned something, anything, about being married to a gay person. *The Other Side of the Closet* nearly jumped off the shelf and into my hands. I read that book as if I were searching for the meaning of life. I went online and did a search for "straight spouse" (a term I found in the book), and I located the Straight Spouse

Network, a worldwide support group (online and face-to-face) for people in my situation. My next move was to find a therapist. These three things changed my life and started me on the road to recovery.

One of the hardest questions from other people that I've had to answer numerous times over the past 10 years was "How could you not have known?" In essence, the person is asking, "How could you be so stupid?" People are also curious about our sex life. My answer: If a person doesn't want you to know, they will do everything within their power to keep you from knowing.

All those questions and thoughts went through my mind, too: How could I *not* know? I knew this man since he was 19 years old. He didn't *look* gay (whatever that means) and he didn't *act* gay, so how could I have known? We had a very normal active marriage. Besides, I always thought people who were married and had children couldn't be gay. It appears that is not the litmus test for gayness. I also thought that gay men didn't have sex with women. Apparently, I was wrong. I asked him once how could he have sex with me if he was gay, and he very coldly said, "A warm body is a warm body." So there it is – straight from the horse's mouth, his harsh truth and my painful reality.

My healing process did not happen overnight. I discovered that the more I shared with others, the lighter my burden became and my fear began to subside. Paul waited a year before coming out to our daughter. By the time he finally told her, she had already figured it out. We took her to counseling to help her cope with our separation and eventual divorce. She was only 14, and it was difficult for her. He wasn't out of the closet to his parents or at work. She was attending a Christian school and didn't feel comfortable talking to anyone about her home situation. In her junior year of high school, she transferred to a public school and felt more comfortable sharing her feelings with friends. She soon discovered that most of them had no adverse response to her disclosure. She is now very open about her father and has no fear of being judged by others.

Our separation and divorce were difficult and rocky. I don't think there is such a good thing as *Happily Divorced*, maybe just "eventually divorced." Divorce is divorce; it is never pretty or fun. I won't get into all the gory details. Suffice to say, we survived that passage of our lives, and everyone came out alive.

As for my continued healing, I eventually told my parents about Paul's coming out a year after our separation, and they were very supportive. I'm now to a point that, if anyone asks about my divorce, I tell them the truth. Imagine that. I feel by sharing my story, I am helping to educate someone's mother, sister, friend, or child about a situation that may happen in their family.

The sad part of this story is that Paul, even though he is now out of the closet, is very unhappy. He has a strained relationship with our daughter and is still very angry with me under his amicable façade. I never could understand why he was so angry. I suppose he feels I should have stayed with him in spite of his preference for men. The day before our divorce was final, he begged me to reconsider. When I asked him if he was still gay…silence. I guess that answered my question.

I have no ill feelings toward him. I understand he didn't choose to be gay, and I'm sure he loved me the best that he could. I wish things could have been different, but they weren't. Someone once told me, "Time heals all wounds," and that used to make me angry. Now, I can see the wisdom in that statement. It's true, and I am living proof of it. After nine years, I can truly say I am happy. I have moved forward in my life. I'm back in school working towards my master's degree, and life is good. My daughter and I have a strong, close relationship. We've not only survived, but thrived. I hope the same for all straight spouses: to some day THRIVE.

After years

Duke…

We met in the former Soviet Union after the fall of communism, both American foreigners teaching at a newly founded university in a newly post-communist republic. I was in my thirties, and she was in her twenties. As history unfolded around us, we found we had had lots of common experiences in Western Europe but had never met there. Now, we'd found each other, and it was all very romantic. We settled into our relationship that would lead to marriage and kids within a few years after returning home.

In the States, she followed me to my grad school, and then I followed to hers. We took turns supporting each other while I completed my dissertation. She got her first job in a Midwest city. A year later, she pregnant with our first child and unhappy in her job, I took a job two states away. Then, a year later, we moved to another state. Four years after that, we moved to yet another state. I'd moved into administration off a tenure track because it was easier to find better jobs as a new academic. Her profession allowed her to work in a job market almost anywhere.

In the meantime, our sex life diminished. She turned down my advances so regularly, I quit trying, letting her take the initiative. She was struggling with depression and slept a lot in the evenings, while I took care of the household and kids. I thought that explained our lack of passion and wanted to be supportive. Moreover, our family was growing, further distracting both of us from sex. Until this partnership, I had been largely debt free, but with needs from pregnancies, transitions, and travel to far-flung family, debts built considerably. We finally bought our first house near the peak of the real estate bubble.

After our last move, my gay wife made friends with a charismatic lesbian couple with children the same age as ours. This was the connection she needed to finally face up to her orientation. When our youngest was two and the oldest, seven, she came out of the closet with me. Within a month or so, I moved out of the bedroom into a spare room and futon. However, I encouraged her to explore this new side of herself and connect with the local community.

In those first months, I prepared for the coming storm. We'd stopped attending Meetings because she didn't shine to it anymore. I went back with the kids to re-establish my local Quaker community connections. She started dating and was either gone or on the phone with her new peers and lovers most of the time. I was left alone, watching over the kids. This was the first Christmas we didn't both take the kids to family. I had a miserable experience outing my wife with my extended family and letting them know the marriage was on the rocks. The kids couldn't fathom what was going on.

Then a cruel twist. I received notice that I would lose my job in six months. There had been misunderstandings during a too-busy transition time after the boss who hired me was fired. I didn't fit in with the rest of the office, with an age gap, different education, and doing work no one else knew how to do. The loss was arbitrary, unfair, and reflected poor judgment. Nevertheless, it shook my confidence in my skills and chosen profession and sent me in a deep depression. All that kept me going was the daily family routine and taking care of the kids.

The job loss required me to move to find a new position. I'm very qualified, but my job market is national, not local. At 50 years old and with rising unemployment, it wasn't a good time to seek a starting level local position. With grief, I looked for and found a job on the East Coast at twice the pay and better responsibilities. I applied, thinking that the city would be attractive to the gay wife, too, (she could make twice the money) so the family wouldn't have to split up. When she said she wouldn't go, I wanted the kids. Unfortunately, there was no time for a custody fight. We hadn't even started divorce proceedings. So I did the hardest thing I've ever done. I left my kids and family behind while we tried to sort out our dispute long distance.

My life didn't go well. I called up every night to help put the kids to bed. My eldest was particularly attached to me and would spend up to an hour or more a night with me. My youngest at three was largely unintelligible on the phone but often tried. The middle boy eventually found the phone too difficult to bother with. When I came back for a weekend, three weeks after departure, I found a big welcome from the kids, but my futon had been carted off for conversion into a desk. The mediation set up didn't help because it could not adjudicate custody, just set up a visiting plan. I never got much good advice from my lawyer, not that any advice could have helped. I just lost money there I didn't have.

The job had me working long hours with little time for socializing. However, I found an SSN face-to-face group that was very welcome. My living circumstances were minimal, a room and shared bathroom. I kept returning to the kids for the first several months, but, eventually, my finances broke. We'd never split up the debts. Between student loans and credit card debt, over a third of my after-tax income flowed. Another third went to pay bills and for the kids. I was also preparing to have them for the summer, needing a proper apartment and accompanying expenses. So bills started to go unpaid.

I had a happy summer with the kids, but work suffered as I couldn't put in the normal long hours with them around. By summer's end, I submitted my resignation, my reasons simple. I was unhappy with the job and work load. I couldn't pay bills and still be regularly with the children. Staying would be permanent exile. I also had no time for social integration in the new city. I had little keeping me there. So I chose the elegant solution: to not pay bills and to return to town, where my social network was weak, but still more vital then where I was, and where family was, even if there were no good job prospects.

My situation went from very bad to even worse. A few days before returning, the gay wife told me I couldn't move back into the house. Her girlfriend was there. Though we were still technically married and my name was on the mortgage, I wasn't welcome. I'd be homeless. The resignation was non-revocable, so I returned, figuring that homelessness and unemployment near the kids were better than continued exile. The lawyer did not recommend conflict, so I lay down and gave up.

A local Quaker family had a spare room in their basement. The gay wife took me up on the offer for child care as my family contribution, which would have been worth around $1400 a month. So, I restarted my daily routine with the kids, and my spirits started on the slow upswing. Later, I moved into the basement of an older lady from the Meeting, earning my keep by helping out around the house, which helps my sense of usefulness though takes considerable time.

Unemployment remains a problem. The local job market at the university is poor, and I didn't get any offer from my applications. I made a few applications for out-of-town jobs, but never got a call back. I pay minimal bills through selling plasma and occasional odd jobs. My own family pays for trips for me and the kids to visit them. I get most of my food from the gay wife and kids' leftovers. I've defaulted on all loans and credit cards. Luckily the gay wife is still financially intact so she uses her credit card so I can get rental cars for travel with the kids.

It's now over a year since I returned. Though I have no job or proper home, I am a daily part of the kids' lives. They do better in school and at home. They are not part of any adult conflict. Their mom works two jobs and maintains the extensive social life she loves. I use the family car in the evenings as needed and, during the day, get about with bike and busses. I enjoy cycling. I indulge myself in reading books for pleasure and some Netflix and Hulu. On a daily basis, my spirits are actually rather good, much better than when I was so far from family. Unfortunately though, career and finances are in ruins. I'd planned to build the resume with volunteer work, but homelessness wrecked my morale. Moreover, the unpaid work of two households has fragmented my time, so major projects for me haven't happened. I've taken on some responsibilities in the Meeting but hesitate to tackle too much. I am unsure of myself.

Technically, we remain married, having never finished the paperwork. For better or worse, dating is lowest priority. Besides being unusually shy, I'm too ashamed of having no job and relying on charity for survival. Moreover, who could believe my story? I hardly do myself. On the positive side, the Meeting has been good for support, and I have my own committee of care. Spiritually, I feel sustained and await new inspiration for the next step in my life.

Madeline...

It's amazing how 30 years of memories can escape you when you find out your husband is gay. You question everything. We had a wonderful life together. It was intimate, adventurous, and sexual. We had three children, meaningful careers, and, most importantly, love. We supported each other...always.

After many years of teaching in Fairfax County middle and high schools, I took early retirement. I loved my work, but there was always so much to do having three children, a husband, and a house. Also for many years, I had had elderly parents who needed attention. I think more than anything else, I wanted to have time for myself to explore.

I was used to having the summer to spend time in the garden, reading, and cooking, so this first summer of retirement was not very different from the others. We went on a Windjammer Cruise; I joined a health club and stayed busy volunteering at a Domestic Abuse Center and "lunching" with friends. However, a subtle change was occurring. I felt very alone and flat.

Christmas came, but I didn't enjoy it. My family got on my nerves. My daughter's boyfriend was late and not suitably dressed. My husband had put on the "Messiah," and I told him sharply that it was inappropriate to have that playing while we were at the table. He immediately turned it off, and I suddenly wanted to cry.

It was all such a contrast to how I usually felt at Christmastime. Everyone I loved was there. The food, music, parties, and decorations have always been far more important to me than gifts, and yet I cannot remember any of it.

A couple of days after Christmas, my husband tactfully said that he thought I needed to see a psychiatrist. He recognized symptoms that I had shown once before, and I agreed. I knew this time I wanted a woman doctor and someone who was nearby. I felt that God was with me. The woman I saw was someone with whom I established rapport easily and quickly. After talking to me for about an hour, she said I was chronically depressed and had suffered from depression all my life. This explained several difficult chapters of my life. Besides medication, she suggested that I have some sessions with a psychotherapist and suggested one.

Once again, I felt that I was in very good hands and have felt well-cared for ever since. It turned out to be providential because of what was going to happen later. Learning to talk to a therapist is not easy. At least it wasn't for me. Especially when she looked at me when I paused and asked, "What are you thinking about now?" It takes concentration and effort to articulate what's going on inside your head. I was very uncomfortable and unable to share my feelings. I realized that my depression made me feel very unsettled. I wasn't sure what I wanted or frankly what I was doing there. I had to find me and that was a gradual process.

Therapy taught me to think about what I wanted and more importantly to be assertive and focus on my wishes and face the future confidently. This helped me to develop confidence in myself. It was just the beginning. It was effective and enabled me to enjoy the following months as I planned a pleasant vacation for myself, my husband, and my younger daughter between Antibes and Juan les Pines on the Riviera with a luxurious way home on the Queen Elizabeth II. It was a belated twenty-fifth wedding anniversary gift to ourselves. In the early days of my family's stay in the U.S., most World Bank employees went home on leave by air and returned by sea, so I had enjoyed several Atlantic crossings. Bob had never had this experience, and I was anxious to relive it.

They say, "You can never go home again." Although I enjoyed many parts of the trip -- the music and dancing lessons were as wonderful as they were before--, it fell far short. My real cause for concern was my husband. It was obvious to me that he was unhappy. A person who had always been able to show enthusiasm suddenly seemed anxious and fearful. We were invited to the Captain's cocktail party. As Bob had chosen for us to sit alone in the dining room, we had not really gotten to know any other passengers. In a crowded room with people, the ship's officers introduced themselves, but, to keep conversation going, it was up to guests to interact. I was quite shocked that Bob, normally outgoing and friendly, was withdrawn. He came to the dance classes and was quite upset when, during the tango, the ship lurched and I tripped over his foot. What provoked him further was my laughing about it. I thought it was funny. Neither of us are great dancers, but we usually enjoyed it. We took a private lesson with the charming Romanian dance instructor, and it seemed to be very important to Bob that we master the tango. Usually dancing had just been fun. But now, for him, it was a challenge.

Even supper was challenging. Every night, he went so far as to order special dishes when the extensive menu would more than satisfy any palate. Of course, all these abnormalities did not come together in my mind at the time. In looking back, they make sense.

When we returned home to Falls Church, Virginia, life fell back into routine. Bob returned to work at his law firm, and I worked in the garden and exercised at the gym. As fall arrived, the Boston Red Sox came to Baltimore to play against the Orioles on Labor Day weekend. Bob's sister, being an ardent fan, flew in for the game. Unfortunately, after we sat in the stands for a very long time, the game was “rained out” and we returned home. The rest of the weekend must have passed pleasantly as we always enjoy Elizabeth’s company, but I have no memory of what we did.

Labor Day Monday changed my life and my thirty-year marriage. Bob drove Elizabeth to DWI to catch her plane, and I stayed home. When he returned, he made us some coffee, and we sat out on the patio by our lily pond. Bob said he wanted to talk. Here, in the prettiest part of our home, surrounded by perennial beds, flowers and shrubs, home to hummingbirds and dragonflies, where I could always come to seek tranquility and come to always feel at peace with the world, he told me that he was gay.

He said he’d suspected it over the last couple of years, and it was only through a men’s organization and through work with his therapist that he’d finally been able to confront it. He explained that when he had driven Elizabeth to the airport, he told her first so I would have somebody with whom to share this and not be isolated. I knew he felt very guilty. He said that he would never leave me unless I gave him permission to do so. I realized that this must be the reason for his strange behavior in the last 6 months. I was so shocked, I couldn’t take it all in. I cried a lot; he cried a lot. He told me I was his best friend. He was genuinely very sad. My world came crashing down!

For several years, I’d been planning the next stage of our lives, researching real estate markets in Maine, looking for a new place to call home and be closer to family. I’d already retired early. Then, it would be Bob’s turn to take a break from his civil service career and work in the private sector for a large corporation. I would be a corporate wife. We would go on a lot of all-expenses-paid trips to well-known flashy resorts. I had it all planned.

So here we sat in silence in my beautiful garden, my sanctuary, and cried. My thoughts were thrashing in a tempest. I was thinking how glad I was that both sets of parents were no longer alive and we didn’t have the burden of telling them. Not a word left my lips as I looked at him, thinking, how could I not have known? I remember turning that question over in my mind and found myself devastated and angry. Did he not realize that I stayed in the US and I did not return to England because of him? Then, I thought of our three children. If I hadn't married him, these beautiful children, aged 28, 24, and 22, would not exist. When we left our garden, I cried the rest of the day. He cried too and comforted me.

I stayed in shock and denial. Even though I sat with my husband who told me he was gay, I didn't believe it. I even told my therapist two days later that I wondered if he were really gay. She suggested that we go on the assumption that he wasn't gay and just talk about any changes in his behavior and my feelings towards him. I left in a thick surreal fog of insecurity.

The next day, I was scheduled to work at the Domestic Violence Shelter office. On the way there, I was listening to what I thought was a story on NPR. I suddenly realized it was a news report. As I drove to the spot where I usually parked, which was just a few miles from the Pentagon, I heard sirens. It was 9-11.

While at TACC, the Temporary Arlington Community Center, I did my best to calm those around me. It was all surreal. I heard the panic, the chaos, and yet was immune. When I left, my mind returned to its usual turmoil. The irony was the ride home. There was no traffic. The back roads on which I traveled were empty. I came and went easily and safely, unlike hundreds of thousands that day. For a long time, I suffered from own private 9-11 and, as horrible as it sounds, I could not focus on the terrible tragedy confronting the public that day. I was numb.

All I could reflect upon was the need for help, for everyone's need for help, for my own need for help. I was crying out and no one could hear me. No one except Elizabeth. She heard my cry and told me about a wonderful support group for men and women whose spouses have come out. It took me a year to join. When I did, I learned that I was one of the fortunate ones whose gay partner had behaved honorably.

How does one define "honorably"? Telling their spouses they were gay rather than their partners' having to find out through various means, often pornographic websites, membership cards to clubs, police knocking at the door, a dildo stashed, and then bearing the emotional burden of having to confront their spouse with those findings only to be lied to continually. What we all shared was that, when our spouses first came out, even if they felt guilty, they were also relieved.

This release made them euphoric and gave rise to what I call "elderly teenager syndrome." My formerly quite preppy husband wore a Utilikilt and brown twill just to work in the garden. He dyed his hair a disastrous color and asked me to shave his back. He took offense at innocent remarks and wanted nothing more to do with our Episcopal church. He was really angry at the Catholic Church but didn't have much for the Episcopalians either, even the liberal ones. He finally shared with me that he preferred to live by himself. This, of course was hurtful despite the fact that some of his antics were irritating me. I suggested that we take a vacation together, Club Med.

One of our best family memories was of a Family Club Med we'd taken in the Bahamas ten years before. We did take this vacation and enjoyed it, but it didn't change his mind. Part of me was hoping the draw to family was greater than gay. It wasn't. He ended up living at home only part time and living with a roommate part time. The atmosphere of our home was doom and gloom. I knew neither of us was happy. I told him if he wanted to move into his own condo, he could.

He was grateful, found a place the following weekend, and moved within just a few weeks.

One thing I'd like to impart is whatever has happened, we need to do our best to be patient with ourselves and not let the effects on us fester and spoil our lives. We have to find ourselves.

Phil...

I continue to be taken aback at how quickly a long-term relationship can unravel. The first inclination of a non-traditional relationship developing was when Tracy started excluding me from activities with Shirley. Since we practically grew up together, a majority of our friends were shared and there never was a feeling of "X is *my* friend and Y is *your* friend." This changed with Shirley. It was great that Tracy had a close girlfriend she was able to open up to, regardless of whether I was included. However, while I never suspected her of having an affair, I developed a mild annoyance to her constant instant messaging with Shirley from her Blackberry. The contents of their communications (email, texts, chats) were always shielded from my view or quickly closed – not that I intended to read them, respecting the privacy of their friendship.

The extent of their relationship became clear during an April holiday we took to Thailand in which Tracy spent the evening before bedtime and the first waking hours corresponding with Shirley. Her careless, unsuccessful email logout led to my viewing several questionable email subjects along the lines of "I love you so much" and "Missing you, baby." This was the first time my mind started to churn and replay events of their relationship. After a bit of sleuthing, I gained unfettered access to their emails and chats, gathering evidence of her affair. I postponed the confrontation until our return stateside, as I wanted to interrupt Tracy joining Shirley on tour (she's an up and coming singer). The allure of the tour outweighed Tracy's excitement over Thailand, and, vindictively, I desired to drop the metaphorical bomb while they were together.

My email indicating awareness of the affair, sent two days into their trip, was answered with phone calls, texts, and emails from Tracy, frantically attempting to contact me -- which I ignored. She returned home on the earliest available flight and began professing how sorry she was, how much she loved me, and she wanted to move back to California and have children.

She provided details of the affair and indicated it had been going on since November.

I realized the affair was complicated, as it had Tracy not only questioning her sexuality, but willing to risk gambling on our strong, loving relationship. I knew her journey to discover her true sexuality would be lengthy and require exploration. Consequently, I tried to be as supportive as possible and initiated two “rules” to guide her: (1) be honest and open and (2) if you’re going to be intimate with Shirley, don’t come home that night. From there, we progressed in the pseudo-happy relationship (laughing, visiting with friends, spending time together, spooning…) – ignoring the elephant in the corner. Over the next six months, Tracy alluded to focusing on determining her sexuality and seeing Shirley on a limited, platonic basis. However, by accessing her email yet again, I learned that their affair had continued.

During Tracy’s six-month “sexual walkabout,” I remained supportive and loving but professed I had no idea how long I could maintain it. This second deception made my decision to invoke a trial separation easier. While she had a lot to sort out, it could no longer be done under the same roof. I could no longer trust she was being “honest and open,” and time away would give me an opportunity to determine what I wanted out of a relationship.

As of November 2010, Tracy continues to be baffled by whether she is gay or straight and is temporarily living with her girlfriend until she takes the initiative to find her own apartment. I live in our apartment and am foraying into the single world after a 14-year hiatus.

Although I have a “good head on my shoulders,” support from others did help in coping with the situation. As soon as I returned from Thailand, I’d searched the Internet for information. Luckily, I quickly found the Straight Spouse Network (SSN) and, within a month, attended my first face-to-face meeting. SSN has been extremely beneficial, proving an outlet for my questions/concerns as well as compassion from those on a similar journey. In addition, I began seeing a therapist bi-monthly (something I'd never considered before) to share my thoughts/feelings as well as obtain guidance in these murky waters. Up to a month ago, these were my only two support outlets because Tracy preferred her lesbian affair be kept under wraps. However, "deception part two" laid the groundwork for me telling three friends and my dad.

I've tried to look on the "bright side" of the recent dogleg my life has taken and see that I am physically and emotionally healthy. I'm a "catch" for someone out there and, at the age of 32, without kids, a whole new life is ahead. There's a great degree of sadness over the potential loss of our fourteen shared years, but I'm looking ahead with enthusiasm on where the next journey will take me. While I don't want to deem our relationship out for the count, with the sensible shoes, four years of softball in high school, affinity for folk music, ability to throw a spiral to rival most guys, and a year affair with a woman, to name a few, the odds are pretty slim.

The recent turn of events have "taken the blinders off" of my view of the relationship. Although she had a successful career, I constantly felt that I put 80% (to her 20%) in our relationship. I was rarely "nurtured" and, hypothetically looking to the future (blatantly ignoring the lesbian issue) and adding children and pets to the mix, I'd probably have run myself in to the ground. Consequently, I've come to terms with the metaphorical sunset of our life together.

Beth…

Peter and I met in 1992 and began dating in the spring of 1995. At the time, I knew he'd had a homosexual relationship that lasted several months the previous summer and fall.

We dated for a year and a half, during which Peter would back off for periods and reconsider whether he wanted to continue the relationship. We didn't explicitly talk of homosexuality. I'm sure it was on his mind, and I was aware of it but also naïve about what internal sexuality forces were moving within him. Peter was seeing a counselor, dealing with past abuse and family issues. His therapy was similar to reparative therapy: Peter looking for ways to minimize his homosexuality and make gay feelings go away or at least be less important.

I re-evaluated whether or not to continue dating him each time he backed off and before we'd continue. I'm glad I did. I kept a journal about the relationship and what I thought and felt. I wasn't trying to manipulate him or trap him into dating or marriage. In fact, I was pretty sure we weren't getting married, because I had plans of moving abroad. Yet I enjoyed our relationship and grew to love Peter. When he first brought up marriage, it was a shift in direction for me but seemed natural. I made the choice that I would rather spend life with this person I loved, than go to a place I wanted to live. We were engaged in 1996 and married three months later.

When we married, he was honest with me and I was honest with myself. We knew we were not just taking a step, but making a giant leap of faith. At the same time, we were naïve.

He believed what he'd heard in therapy and through many ex-gay groups: with enough hard work, his gay feelings would eventually lessen, if not disappear, altogether. I believed what he told me that was going on in his heart and mind. I also trusted in his character enough to believe that he would make good choices about me. We knew that it was a risky venture. We did not know, as no 24- and 22-year-old can know, how weighty those risks would feel when we had been married for 14 years and had added three children to our family. We didn't know we'd be in our late 30s and realize no one else we knew of had made it and that we were doing the "impossible."

Three months plus ago, my husband told me he is gay. For me, this was a huge difference and shift in who we were. I am no longer married to a man who struggles with homosexuality. I am married to a gay man. Although it was not brand new information, it is my "disclosure" moment and the starting point of our post-disclosure world. I learned that Peter's struggle with homosexuality had intensified. The thoughts and feelings had not gone away and were more intense. Over the years, his struggle against such an integral part of himself had become self-hatred and recently had become too costly to him as a person. Just prior to disclosure, he'd considered suicide.

We didn't get from marriage to disclosure overnight. There were steps and choices along the way. Two years into our marriage, I found gay porn on Peter's computer. When I asked him about it, his first response was a lie: the porn was there because a co-worker had used his computer. Within a few days, he told me the truth – it was his file I'd seen.

That admission made a lot fall into place. For the first time, I knew what it was to have gut feelings proven true. It was empowering to know I wasn't imagining something or falsely accusing my husband. It was horrible to realize how easily he could lie to me and that there had been other untruths along the way.

We began marriage counseling. Through that process, we developed a policy that we refer to as our own "Don't ask, don't tell." DADT began so that I wasn't involved in "policing" my husband's actions or holding him accountable for his commitments. I wanted him to be accountable desperately but also wanted him to have integrity and be committed to me and "us" by his own choice. I didn't want him to shape his behavior because he was afraid I'd check up on him or of my response if I caught him in something. In our DADT, Peter had the responsibility to set up relationships in our church and circle of friends with straight men. The relationships would include accountability related to porn use and any other actions related to homosexuality. We agreed he would tell me if his temptation ever got to be too much or if he "acted out" on his gay feelings.

It felt unfair that all the decisions rested with Peter. At first, I felt I'd lost some element of control because I couldn't ask him about whether or not he was using porn or how his struggle with homosexuality was going. I soon realized that a feeling of control was an illusion, anyway. This was something internal within him, and the decisions *did* rest with him, fair or not. Our new policy, as I got used to it, also freed me to be able to trust that he was working on the issues. There was emotional freedom as I realized I didn't have to be part of ensuring that he followed through on his commitments to me.

After disclosure, I found out that Peter had continued to use porn, mostly during periods of stress. At this point, logically, it was "small potatoes," not a major worry. Emotionally, it was loaded with meaning, and I was upset. To find out he'd been doing something "gay" all along highlighted how little I knew of what was going on in him and the choices he made throughout our marriage. His hidden porn use demonstrated how easily he could hide something, particularly if he knew I was trying to trust him and choosing not to search into what he was doing. On the other hand, he'd followed through with our agreements about accountability. His men's group knew of his porn use, and he'd sought support from them when he used the porn.

Over the years, Peter has been faithful. He has not had sex outside the marriage. My sole verification of that is my trust in him. I'm very aware, by learning more of goings-on in mixed marriages, that virtually all gay men I've heard about cheat on straight wives. So I could be naïve and trusting.

I've also had to look at my choices: trust him and the character he's shown throughout our relationship or not trust him and spend my life looking for clues that prove me right. Frankly, that second option seems exhausting and self-defeating, so I am choosing trust. As I connect with other wives in mixed marriages, I am cautious of describing this choice. Many husbands in these marriages have secret lives and are so disconnected from themselves, much less their wives, that they have destroyed the trust given to them and not made changes to earn back any level of confidence. They are not Peter, who has disclosed his attractions and feelings about homosexuality and has worked on understanding himself and his sexuality throughout our marriage.

Now that Peter's accepted he's gay, we've talked again about DADT and don't know if it was beneficial or harmful overall. Benefits include relative peace, during which homosexuality was not a front-burner issue for most of the marriage. By comparison, in our post-disclosure world, "gay" seems to be all we talk about. At first, we focused on, cried over, fought about, and discussed his sexuality and what this change means. Lately, gay issues and gay culture are virtually always part of our conversation. I sometimes miss my blissful [chosen] ignorance. But, DADT worked only while Peter was in the closet-- and that is no longer an option. Nor would I want it to be.

I now have an inkling of how dark and painful that closet was. He's told me how isolated and lonely it felt to not be able to talk about his homosexuality with me. As he came more into that identity, the closet meant that he met gay feelings with fear and tried to push them away. That was dangerous and unhealthy for his sanity.

Now, I am unpacking 14 years' worth of my doubt and fear that I never felt I could express. Another result of DADT is that Peter wouldn't share what was going on deep in him. I was looking for what was deep in his thoughts, his spirituality, and his other relationships – not wanting to go to the level of sexuality because it was personally painful, but still wanting to know about him. He would hear me ask about his heart and realize he couldn't talk about what was deepest to him. Likewise, all his energy was spent managing his gay feelings, so he didn't have much capacity left to love or emotionally pursue me or try to get to know me at the deepest levels. Our relationship wasn't superficial, but it lacked depth in areas of self-disclosure. We both have pain over not having felt pursued by our partner to know the deepest parts of our heart. The relative "peace" I had during these last 12 years was costly.

There were times during our DADT that Peter discussed temptations with me or came very close to choosing to have sex outside the marriage. Each admission threw me into a tailspin for a few days, overcome with anxiety and feeling I could no longer trust Peter. He had made faithful choices, but hearing of the temptations and thinking of the "what if's" reminded me that a huge threat to our marriage always loomed just out of sight.

The times of temptation were a threat because I'd decided early on that infidelity would mean the end of our marriage. Peter knew that was my position. In the years since, I saw marriages that recovered after infidelity and understand it is possible. I've wondered if my decision was based more on the idealism and inflexibility of someone in her 20s. However, given our mixed-orientation status now, I know that this is still a boundary that is vital to me. Trust is very fragile in our world, and I don't believe I could take on the work of rebuilding it.

Now that we have an understanding of our marriage as one of mixed-orientation, we've realized there are some interesting definitions of what is and is not "sex" in an MOM. Some couples phrase the meaning of "sex" very finely, in order to say that they are monogamous or that they are not having outside sex, even when having physical same-sex relationships. A recent online discussion of the issue prompted Peter and I to be very explicit with each other about our own definition – a broad definition: Erotic touch = sex; Orgasm, ejaculation by whatever means = sex; Oral contact with body parts = sex. I'm glad the issue came up. Through our conversation, we found we were on the same page, agreeing with each other on a "sex is sex" type of definition.

My life in the last almost four months has been a rollercoaster. It is amazing how much has changed and how quickly. I used to measure everything in weeks: "On this day, 2 weeks ago, the bottom dropped out of my life and everything changed." Eventually, time stretched a little further, and I realized it wasn't helpful to constantly think back to what used to be in our lives. We're never going back. I'll never again have a husband in the closet. That is for the better. Now the question is whether or not remaining married is also for the better.

Early on after disclosure, Peter became very defensive and angry, feeling that divorce was inevitable, and would talk of it often. We fought often and had heartbreaking conversations. I was angry at him, defensive over feelings he was planning to leave me. I also felt anger that he had betrayed commitments to me. I didn't believe that he had been physically unfaithful but that his change in how he identified himself was a betrayal of the life we had together. I told him he was a stranger to me. There had been so much internal work in him that was totally hidden. And, so much was new in his outlook and personality, that he *was* a stranger.

As Peter took on and embraced his new identity, it consumed most of his thoughts and all our conversations. It also meant he had little emotional energy left for empathy. He tried. Nonetheless, some thoughtless comments he made seared in my brain. As he worked out our new world after the DADT policy was lifted, he learned that there are still things you don't say out loud. Some things in a relationship you choose not to say out of compassion or empathy for your spouse. Likewise, some things I try to forget out of love for Peter.

We processed through so much new territory – questions of how to relate to each other. What would our future hold? Could we stay together? Were we lunatics to think that we could stay together when so many could not? Was divorce inevitable? Things we thought yesterday were null and void by the time we were able to talk again today.

Young children in the house meant that much of our time together was forced on family life, rather than our own drama. I am grateful for the distractions and also ashamed for the way the children were on autopilot through a large part of the summer. They didn't get enough of me, but they got everything I had to give.

Two months post-disclosure, we made contact with a couple we had known years before. We knew that she was straight and he was gay. On the way to have dinner with them, we didn't know if we would find out that they were happy or unhappy, if they were monogamous or had an open marriage. Our dinner turned into a five-hour non-stop conversation. Jack and Penny have been married for more than 20 years. Gay, he has remained faithful to her. She loves him and respects him without reservation. She loves the fact that he is gay – it's what shaped him and made him who he is. Throughout the night, she said, "I'm straight. He's gay. So what? We love each other." He echoed the sentiment. He also discussed costly choices they made. She agreed. A mixed marriage is hard. But – every marriage has choices and trade-offs. Every person, gay or straight, is tempted to unfaithfulness. Both of them consistently used language that put choices they'd made in context. They wouldn't let it be about "the gay thing," but discussed the costs in any marriage. They remembered the pain they felt early on in their post-disclosure journey. It hasn't all been easy.

It was invaluable for us to see a couple who had remained faithful to each other in a MOM and had a good life together. We left the dinner with a new understanding of how we might work out a new hope that divorce wasn't inevitable. Most importantly, we left with friends and allies to call on as resources. The whole meeting was pivotal. Immediately afterwards, we had five days away from kids and day-to-day responsibility to talk through some of our hopes and fears for our future.

We found that there are things for which we need affirmation in every day. Peter needs to know that I know he's gay and that I love and accept him. I do, but it's a change. I no longer "put up with" him being gay or wish it would go away. I know he's gay and love that about him. I love the person he is – and he's gay. We've also come to realize that Peter needs to know that I believe he is doing the best he can. He needs to know I don't think he's a villain who's manipulated me into and in this marriage. And, as his transition began, I did hold him responsible: he was the one making a change; he was wrong; his orientation was incompatible with our marriage. I no longer think that. He is not wrong for following this path to greater health and wholeness. Gay is not "wrong."

These post-disclosure months have not been a linear progression, but a big muddle. One way I sort through the muddle is physical. I'm a runner. I've run almost every day since disclosure. I've discovered that sobbing can mess up my breathing and cut a run short. Anger really messes up my pacing. I also find I often have a better understanding of myself and our situation at the end of a run. Some runs have been a way to put feet to my feelings of wanting to escape. I run it out and can come back to my day and take care of my kids. Some runs have been to quiet my brain when I couldn't stop the endless loops of fear or pain.

In the same way, I've found a lot of peace and truth in practicing yoga. The sayings that apply to how to move my body in practice often apply in life: "Lead with your heart, not your head" and "Be present."

Since Peter identified himself as gay (as opposed to "struggling"), I have felt anger, betrayal, and fear. I'm angry over change that's out of my control and about betrayal – that his commitments to me have changed. I fear the extent of further changes and what lies ahead for me and my kids.

Meanwhile, my questions have changed. An early unspoken one was "Can't we just go back to what we used to have?" Soon enough, I wanted to know if he had a boyfriend or had been unfaithful. Did an event or person trigger this change? As I got more in touch with my feelings, I realized that I was questioning myself. I wanted to know what it meant for me, about me, to me to have a gay husband. It wasn't a question of what others thought. I wondered what I was missing out on, compared to a straight marriage. I wondered what parts of myself I had stifled or changed in order to be part of this mixed-orientation marriage. Were there elements of female sexuality I'd traded in order to be part of this partnership? I questioned physical intimacy, wondering if he wanted *me* or if I was just an available second choice.

I've become more comfortable with owning up to the fact that he does want something other than what I am. But –he also wants me. This continues to be a touchy subject, but one we're working through. As a side note, we have had throughout an active and good sex life.

I need to know that Peter loves me, to hear daily that he intends to stay in our marriage and stay faithful. I need daily words and physical contact that show me he is physically attracted to me. I hate the neediness this situation causes in me. I hate that I need daily affirmation to stay out of the dark places and downward spirals of fear for our future. But, that is where I am now.

As we learn more of the world of gay/straight marriages and venture into the world where gay is embraced, rather than hated and feared, new needs have emerged. I need Peter's understanding as I rail about all the stories I read of horrible deception and injustices in mixed marriages. I need his openness and willingness to allow me to know and question who his friends are. I need to be part of his coming out. I need him to understand my fear of these changes and my slowness to accept some of them. I'm very sensitive to his coming out to gay men now, though I don't believe this will always be the case. Our current agreement is that Peter doesn't make new gay friends without my awareness.

Peter is working though a grieving process related to the type of life he will lead. He has determined to remain faithful to me and will not have sex with a man while we are married. That requires giving up something. He has also found ways of gay self-expression that are not physical intimacy with a man. He's changed the way he dresses, is more conscious of what he eats and his workouts at the gym, and is more involved in LGBTQ causes and activism.

I am choosing to enjoy Peter's gay expression of himself. For the most part, it's easy. I get the benefit of the gym-rat with a smokin' hot physique. I am committed to making gay friends as a couple and opening up our world (but not our marriage) to gay friends. At the same time, I have to do some internal work on trusting Peter. The lie about the porn early on was a turning point at which he decided that he'd tell me the truth. I need to believe in his trustworthiness and not let mistrust and fear kill our marriage. This requires giving up a certain measure of self-protectiveness.

We do have wounds. We have hope. We have a long way to go. But, we have decided that this risky path is one we want to be on. The same leap of faith we took 14 years ago is still the faith required to believe we'll make it now. We know more now about the weight of those risks. Do I know we'll make it? No. Do I believe it's worth trying? Yes.

Crawford...

It had been a tough couple of years, but I chalked it up to the general ebb and flow of family life. We'd brought three beautiful little girls into the world in a span of just over four years. My intellectual wife had been home with them since our middle daughter was born. I figured this time away from her teaching job and the isolation so many stay-at-home parents feel had led her into a state of near depression.

Things had begun to come together as we drove a stretch of one of many suburban freeways on our way to the Billy Joel/Elton John concert in the spring of 2009. I finally asked, "Is any of this related to you regretting marrying a man?" She was taken aback and said she'd not thought about that. She was awkward and speechless, rare for this Ivy League-educated woman.

An analytical type, I looked for signs of what could be wrong in our marriage. When she dyed her hair bright pink, I took it at face value. Born and raised in Berkeley, she didn't fit the mold of the typical, minivan-driving soccer mom. She has a gift of relating equally well to people at fancy cocktail parties and to the pierced and tattooed baristas making coffee at the local Starbucks. Her upbringing in the private school, high society set, combined with the edge from her coming of age as her older sister came out as a lesbian to their conservative parents, was an attractive quality The pink hair was a statement to the rest of the country, not something to disrupt our marriage.

But the fan fiction issue was a bigger issue. She'd been a big fan of fiction, devouring Harry Potter books and movies, and made the leap from this regular form of popular series to online fan fiction. It began with stories of alternate endings and transitioned into reading and writing gay erotica based on the lead characters, creating an alternate online identity, critiquing and commenting on others' stories. The fan fiction lead to many disagreements and a home and children lacking in care as she prioritized the online world above them, her "real life" friends, and, most importantly, our marriage. I felt it was a passing distraction like the time years earlier, when she'd become borderline addicted to her favorite baseball team's fan forum. I had no idea about the relationship blossoming, as our marriage wilted.

Many details are a blur, but I recall discovering an email address as I was getting driving directions on Google. I clicked on the logged-in email to see communications that included giving her cell phone number to people on the fan fiction site. I confronted her on this, and she became angry and defensive that I'd read these emails and break her trust. On another occasion, I walked into our office as the girls watched her typing an email that provided her cell phone number to a stranger. I became angry with her in front of the girls, and the oldest said, "Mommy can do what she wants. You are not in charge of her."

Truer words were never spoken. As much as I wanted to be in charge, I had no control over this woman or my fate. She began to receive mail from one of her online friends and invited me to read what she was reading, but I declined, having no interest in gay erotica.

I began to withdraw, happier at work than when I got home. Things were getting to a desperate place. She wrote me a seven-page letter, pointing the finger at me for not paying enough attention to her, being too focused on work, and not embracing the parts of her that were alternative. She accused me of being oversensitive to what was happening online and making improper allegations that something inappropriate was happening behind my back.

I'd come too close to the truth. Like a cornered pit bull, she was ready to devour me if I dared threaten what she had in her online world. We tried for a reconciliatory trip to Sea Ranch. I hoped the escape would rekindle the flame between me and this incredibly passionate and beautiful woman. She was distracted the whole weekend, struggling with her two disparate worlds. It left me empty and sad.

I knew she'd started therapy and smiled a premature victory smile when she came home with her therapist's recommendation to read How to Become an Adult. A day or two after she told me not to tell her parents about the therapist, she pulled me into our bedroom to talk. There, she shared her struggles and fears of being a gay woman and a mother in a straight relationship.

Thanks to a friend's recommendation to listen to Thich Nhat Han's Art of Mindful Living, I was somehow in another world when she told me. Instead of my default reaction of anger and fear, I responded from a place of love and compassion. We'd gone through a marriage seminar at church that discussed the idea of each spouse being safely known, and I guess we had finally gotten to that point. I told her I'd give her time to figure it out, and we would look at all our options. We cried together and held each other.

The following week, the details slowly, painfully came out. She tried to spin her actions in a positive light, but friendship with this woman who lived a thousand miles away was not run of the mill. She had fallen head over heels in love. But she canceled a planned meeting with her at a Fan Fiction convention and said she would quit the online world. Then, without telling me, she got back into it and said she was going to write one last fan fiction story to help her close the book on this period of her life. I agreed reluctantly, thinking I was doing the right thing and that she was holding my heart in her hands.

Curiosity killed the cat. When I found the story on our computer, I learned it was not for her therapy, it was for this woman. I was so angry at this final lie. To learn your spouse has repeatedly betrayed you is extremely difficult to overcome, especially for me, as I constantly had a hunch something was wrong, repeatedly questioned, and was repeatedly told I was crazy.

Turns out I was right. My incredibly accurate perceptive ability was intact.

One of the biggest issues is that I was one of the last to know. Most of our friends were mutual, and she'd told nearly every one of them about her struggles. It was a lonely place. When I told my closest buddies over a few beers, one of them nearly cried as he told me his wife had shared with him what was happening. He was stuck between a rock and a hard place.

The lies and betrayal were more difficult than the fact she was coming out. We talked around and around about it and, from what I read, this was one of the less damaging scenarios since no physical contact was ever made. Still, it hurt. Trusting someone and finding out you are wrong to trust is one thing. Trusting someone, eventually questioning this trust, being told repeatedly that you are wrong to question the trust, questioning your own abilities to properly perceive a situation, and then learning you were actually correct is another level. It will take me a long time to trust a woman again.

She and I found online boards for people in mixed-orientation marriages and went to counseling, I went to in-person meet-ups with straight spouses, and we talked more than we had for years, using the boards as conversation starters as we tried to determine how far we'd stretch our definitions of marriage. I considered things I never thought I would. We watched the movie, *For the Bible Tells Me So*, about the struggles of five gay people and how Scripture is used inappropriately to support people's fear and hatred. The story that hit closest to home was that of Bishop Gene Robinson. We are Episcopalian and had followed his rise as the first openly gay bishop in the Episcopal Church. In one scene, his wife said the best way she knew to live out her marriage vows was to release him from those vows to allow him to reach his full potential. It was an interesting take, one my wife wished I'd adopt. I felt that if our marriage was going to end because of her desire to be with a woman, then she needed to be the one to leave.

This hurdle extended our struggle, as she hoped I would "release her" and I hoped she would wake up and realize what she had. She finally declared we needed to divorce. I didn't fight it, as I was tired of resisting the inevitable. I'm worth more than having to convince or sell a woman to be with me. While my desire would have been for her to stay and us to piece our family back together, this is best for us both. I'm nervous and apprehensive about the girls.

My wife of nine years moved out in June and settled in a two-bedroom condo around the corner. We told the girls a week in advance, and the reaction was less dramatic than I expected. However, tears ensued with reckless abandon the following day and days after. They are still adjusting to their new reality, and I miss them terribly when they are with their mom. Initially, I did a good job of focusing on myself through therapy, meditation, and concerts, a love of mine that had fallen by the wayside. (We both realized that, in future relationships, we'll do a better job of maintaining some level of autonomy and at least one hobby that nourishes our individual passion.)

Then, the pendulum swung the other way. Every night I didn't have the kids, I went out with a different female friend. But dating existing friends in this state of mind is not the smoothest way to enter into this new world. I've now found a middle ground and enjoy some time focused on myself and some enjoying the company of a woman, if nothing else, to understand how that feels again.

I am cautiously optimistic. The finances scare me, concern of whether or not potential mates would look at my three girls as "extra baggage" hangs over my head, and dealing with my parents is a burden. After I told them, they cleared their house of all pictures that included my soon-to-be-ex-wife, refused to see her or talk to her, and influenced other family members to shy away from doing things with us. That leaves me on an island, trying to do what is in the best interest of my three girls by continuing to have dedicated family time. Beyond these concerns, I have a positive outlook. I am a great catch for the right woman and I now have an opportunity to reach my full potential as a human being.

Carolyn...

It's been a very long time since I've told my story. I was just 22 years old when I married in 1971. I'm 63 and have no children. In hindsight, I always felt there was "something wrong with me." It took me years to learn there wasn't. I cried myself to sleep many a night after we were married. I still suffer from low self-esteem and am grateful for my friends who remind me I matter. I refer to my now ex-husband as TGO, the gay one.

We met in college, sophomore year. The irony is that we were chemistry lab partners with no real sexual chemistry. We became friends. He started out as a French major and switched to International Studies. I studied Political Theory. I used to joke that he thought I was the ugliest, therefore the smartest, girl in the class. We didn't really "date" seriously until junior year, when I returned from visiting my Foreign Service family in Manila, the Philippines, and had lost tons of weight. I was a virgin and didn't know anything, so I never did question why he didn't pursue me sexually nor seem to need or want intimacy. I was lonely often. He was all I knew. He used to joke that he was a "cold fish," but I thought it was a polite excuse and somehow he just didn't want me. We shared a room second semester of senior year in off-campus housing. He slept in the bed, and I slept on a mattress on the floor. I never knew until years later that this was not normal for a straight man. We never had sex until after we were formally engaged and I'd (unbeknownst to my parents) been to Planned Parenthood for my first internal exam, the Pill, and contraceptive foam. And, the first time, he didn't want to touch or kiss my breasts. After we were married, our sex life never evolved. It was always so-so. It was mechanical at best. He always rushed to the bathroom immediately afterwards to wash. I never felt really loved.

The 90's were the defining decade for TGO. It was here that he decided to hitchhike on the road to self-discovery. He quit a good government job with high bucks and a great retirement to become a travel agent. He was a wild gun: job hopping, drinking, and trying to ignore a barrage of serious health problems. When I finally confronted him, he went to the doctor and AA. When he got fired from yet another job, he finally went to therapy and got anti-depressants.

There was no intimacy between us. We were stoic roommates. We even slept in separate bedrooms. We both excused it away with his sleep apnea. I always thought there was more to it, as I think he felt more comfortable in his own space. I kept "hanging in there" as the "good wife" because I made the promise "in sickness and in health." I kept wondering if it would ever be "my turn" to realize true happiness.

We started joint marriage counseling, and I asked him in our second year if he was gay. Of course, he said no. We stuck with therapy nearly eight years. It was difficult to handle the stress, day and night. I never got a break. I had a very high pressure job with the USG, and what should have been my "resting place" wasn't. My marriage was a polar ice cap with no communication and no intimacy. The only positive that came out of therapy was that there were fewer fights between us. I felt tacitly forced by him to withdraw, becoming more and more isolated at home, no friends and no social life. I became a couch potato. I had no emotional or physical energy. My house was falling apart around me.

By the turn of the century, there wasn't prosperity; however, there was closure. It was the perfect storm. All the elements of catastrophe were brewing far beyond my control, and I was at sea, vulnerable. It was the year of the computer, web surfing for porn, and email exchanges. He couldn't run from himself anymore. I came home from work and found a print out by the computer. It was an email exchange about meeting someone for coffee. There wasn't anything sexual. It described when he could get away unnoticed. I discussed this with our therapist, and then I confronted him with it and asked him, "Are you gay?"

And he said, "Well, I think I'm bi." We kept talking; we didn't argue. Then he added, "I may be gay. I'm definitely bi, and I was too scared to tell you because I was afraid you'd leave me."

To which I replied, "We've been living as brother and sister for at least ten years in separate rooms, why would I leave you now?"

We continued counseling about that discovery. That day was a great aha moment – IT'S NOT ME.

The next months were a blur. I remember being asked often in therapy, "What do you want?" I didn't know what to say; I hadn't a clue. By summer, I finally found an answer. I realized I wanted to be "loved, honored, and cherished" just like in the wedding vows and the way I'd done for him through thick and thin for 31 1/2 years. He answered honestly that he didn't think he was capable of doing it. That was it. We agreed we needed to split. There were no arguments, just overwhelming sadness.

By the fall, TGO moved out, I found the Straight Spouse Network, read Amity's book, joined both a face-to-face and an online listserv support group, and tried to muster the strength to meet people in my shoes. I desperately wanted to find the strength to go to an SSN "Gathering," and I did. I found a place to release, heal, talk, listen, and reflect. I can tell you the connection saved my life and gave me the strength to focus on the house. By Feb 2003, our separation agreement was signed. In May 2004, our divorce was final.

So, how's life been since? I've grown bold and beyond my expectations in my new role with the Straight Spouse Network, doing interviews and taking a position on the Board of Directors. It gives me purpose and hope. I continue to suffer loss on many levels: my dear friend died, TGO had a stroke, and I did, too, in 2005.

I'm seven years post-divorce and still don't know where I am emotionally. Rereading my own story makes me angry. I have supreme confidence in myself as an intelligent, articulate person. I have no confidence in myself as a woman. You can be chastised with good intentions. Many people recently have been nagging me to stop isolating myself and to get out of my condo more frequently, if only for a short time. Yet I cannot bring myself to do that. Didn't I say that the word "help" is hard to utter? I know intellectually that I need to go back to counseling. Emotionally, I can't bring myself to do it. Health issues are always there. Although I do almost everything the doctors ask, my lack of movement makes it more difficult to move. It's a catch 22, I know.

The Washington Post interviewed me back in 2008. I tried to tell them how the gay thing has affected my life. I tried to tell them how I felt. I coined a term I call "retroactive humiliation." It's that embarrassment that washes over you when you look back at photographs or you are struck by a memory and you wonder what, if anything, from that time was real. (See http://www.washingtonpost.com/wpdyn/content/article2009/11/06AR2009110602953.html).

I discovered at age 62 that I'm important, I matter, and I deserve the life that's waiting for me whatever I determine it will be. I have no real vision for me. Isn't that sad? I do what I can to help others, but what do I do to help myself?

I would so like to know what it's like to be loved passionately and physically. I don't want marriage. Heck, I can't ever imagine living with someone. I'm a real introvert; I get my energy from being alone. It would be wonderful to have someone occasionally care about me. One can't do what one can't do.

What's one piece of advice I can offer? TALK-TALK-TALK-TALK-TALK! Laugh as much as you can. Realize and really know that it isn't you and that this happens to millions of others. If you can, do what you feel comfortable doing to change the mores of the world so it happens to fewer and fewer of us.

Don't blame yourself! It isn't you! Don't avoid professional help. Get medical and talk therapy. Depression and anxiety medications are not a sign of weakness. Don't hide! (I wish I could take my own advice.) If you get to a point where you are at risk of hurting yourself, check yourself into a hospital and get the help you need.

If you're a straight spouse, you need to tell your story and to help others through the fire. Do have honesty and integrity; they're the key. Communication is critical. Personal relationships are critical. Don't let misunderstandings fester; get them out in the air and try to resolve them. If you can't, let them and the people go! Don't brood about things you can't change. Live your life as honestly as you can. Trust your gut!

Syd...

In 2004, my wife had a scare when they discovered a pre-cancer cell on her skin. Luckily, it had no adverse effects, but it shook her up. Looking back, I wonder if that may have caused her to re-consider her place in life.

2005 started off a good year. My wife and I had been married over 34 years. Our son was grown and out on his own. We had time and money to spend time doing things together that we both enjoyed. Our life was happy, content. We didn't fight or argue. We had busy but rewarding work lives and a physically intimate relationship. I loved her and told her often. I had no doubt about our marriage or our relationship.

Midyear, I noticed she'd become more distant and closer to a young woman who we both considered a friend and had known for about ten years. This woman was on the board of directors of a Catholic high school where my wife was a teacher, and she was an open lesbian. She had serious emotional problems, aggravated by the recent breakup of her long relationship with her female partner and the death of her father. My wife was 55. This woman was 32. I thought my wife was being a good friend, almost motherly, during these tough times.

As the year progressed, my wife became "short" with me over minor issues, something she'd never done. It shocked me. No matter what I said, it was wrong. One day in early September, when we were with friends, I noticed my wife had separated herself from the group and rejected our attempts to include her in the social activity. She seemed annoyed with us and me in particular. When the other woman showed up, my wife literally jumped from her seat and ran down the hill to greet her. They did not walk back to the group. Instead, they went for a walk. I remember thinking that something was very wrong. The word "lesbian" entered my mind, but I quickly dismissed that thought. They came back to the group, and my wife introduced her to everyone as "my best friend in the whole world." These words hurt. She'd always told me I was her best friend in the world; her rock.

On September 6, I celebrated my 60th birthday at home with my wife and the other woman, whose birthday was the next day. I will never forget the card my wife gave me. It said, "The very best is yet to come. Let this year begin the best of times for us. Lots of Love, _____"

I also received a card from the other woman, which read, "Wishing you every happiness and all life's wonderful things. Your friend, ___"

During the evening, they both had their feet up on the coffee table and their feet were touching. I tried to convince myself that it was nothing. On October 16, my wife went out with the other woman for one of their evening walks. When she did not return after several hours, I called to see if she was okay but did not get an answer. She called later that night and said they'd stopped for coffee and then went to her friend's house and dozed off. When she came home, I was awake in bed. I could hear her taking a shower. I was feeling confused, alone, angry, and sad.

For the next several nights, she remained out later and later, sometimes until 1 or 2 AM. I was frantic. I knew something was terribly wrong. I finally felt so anxious that I had to go out and walk. I walked in circles for hours. I could not think straight. On October 20, I gave my wife a letter, written at work. It said I didn't understand what was happening and why we were getting further apart while she and her friend were getting closer together.

After reading it, she said something like: "I've become very fond of Charlotte and we have expressed our affection in every human way possible." She said she'd felt this way for this woman for the past ten years.

I stood in shock, unable to believe this was really happening. I remember holding my hands over my face and saying, "Oh my God, this can't be real." I remember crying and asking her to tell me what had I done. I'd do anything; I'd go to counseling.

My wife replied that I was trying to control her. I begged for a chance to make up for anything I did wrong. She refused to talk. From that time forward, the girlfriend would drive up to the house and pick my wife up. I was in so much pain, I couldn't think straight. I kept saying that this could not be real. I didn't try to stop them. I was frozen, unable to act. All I could do was watch her leave. I remember thinking that she was acting like a teenager with her first love. For several weeks, I didn't eat or sleep. I lost weight, dropping to about 125 pounds. I went to work day after day and tried to hide it. I didn't feel I could tell anyone. They wouldn't believe me. People noticed I wasn't myself, but no one asked to help. I closed the door to my office, unable to stop crying. I wanted to end my life quietly. I felt like a failure. I felt embarrassed that I'd lost everything. I wanted to die and made one, poorly executed attempt, which failed.

I spent my evenings on the computer, looking up any web site that might explain what happened. That's where I found the

Straight Spouse Network. I went to a meeting, thinking they could show me how I could put my marriage back together. I learned that the odds were against that. I saw how devastating this was to other people. They all suffered through the same things I was feeling. My nerves were raw. I continued to walk around in a depressed state. I not feel like life was worth living. One person at work realized I was in trouble and took me to see a doctor, who decided I needed to be hospitalized. I called one of the people from SSN. I could not believe that she dropped everything and sat with me for hours in the waiting area of the hospital. I remember she told me I looked like hell. I am sure I did.

I went to several counselors, none of whom understood or could help. Instead, they said it took two to break up a marriage, making me continue to wonder what I'd done to cause this to happen and to come up with plenty of reasons. One asked who I thought was the "male" in my wife's new relationship. Strange what people ask when they are unfamiliar with the situation!

The only people who understood what I felt were people in SSN. They understood the depression, the anger, the profound sadness, the hopelessness, the self-blame, the denial, the feeling of total betrayal. They knew that nothing I did could cause her to change her sexuality. It took me a long time to finally believe it. The greatest value of meeting other straight spouses was realizing I was not the only person this ever happened to.

My wife and I continued to live in the same house. She continued to see her girlfriend and talk to her by phone for hours. I was still under the delusion we could reconcile. I loved her even though she showed nothing in return. We barely spoke. We were never intimate again. I spent several years on different antidepressants, avoiding friends, staying alone much of the time.

The fourth year after my wife came out, I finally made headway. I stopped blaming myself and denying the reality and finality of the situation. I began to accept it was over. I found new friends and began a slow process of re-socialization (though I kept my story a secret from most people). Recently, someone special came into my life, a woman who is loving, caring, and beautiful. I was able to feel love again. I was able to trust again, even though I swore I would never trust anyone ever again. Now I feel happiness again. I feel so fortunate to have her in my life.

I've decided to file for divorce and begin my life again. At times, I sill feel angry towards my wife for lying, breaking her promises, breaking up our family, her behavior, and betraying my trust. But the overwhelming pain I felt has faded and no longer controls my life.

Cheryl…

It's been over three and a half years since my world came crashing down with the gay episode that ultimately ended my marriage and destroyed the family I had so carefully created. I'm calmer and feel I can put it in perspective.

SK and I met in 7th grade chorus. He played the piano, and I was the teacher's pet. We both were also classroom aides and would race to her class every day, trying to be the first one to get the chair with wheels – a race for the "rolly" every day. We laughed together, teased each other, and began years of performing together.

We spent the rest of our school years in close company through our music. He was a fabulous pianist, and I loved to sing. By our senior year in high school, he was Class President and I, Vice President. He was the Sterling Scholar in music, and I was the runner up. We sang a song he wrote at our high school graduation. He was always a few steps ahead of me. He got perfect grades. I got good grades. He was the life of the party. I was quiet and supportive. I loved his vibrant and enthusiastic approach to life. Left to my own devices, I'd stay cuddled up with a good book for hours. He brought me out of my shell and made me engage with life and friends.

We started dating exclusively the summer after our junior year. We'd sit in his car and talk so late that my mom flashed the kitchen light on and off letting me know she was not ok with that. Little did she know. Nothing was going on inside the car except for great conversation.

SK was gay, and I was too innocent at the time to know anything was other than it should be. We were both raised Mormon. I rarely heard the gay word mentioned much less had any conversation about it. Years later, SK told me, when he was in 5th grade, he said to his mother one day after school, "I think I might be gay." She had swiftly slapped him across the face and told him never to say that again. So, over-achiever that he is, he proceeded to do everything in his power to put gay behind him and be the best young Mormon boy he could be. After graduation, he went on a Mission, and I wrote letters and prayed for him while he was gone. We got married in the Salt Lake Mormon Temple a year after he returned. I had no idea what I was really getting into. We were going to be sealed for time and all eternity in the temple, and I was sure the Lord would help us overcome whatever hurdles we encountered.

I was in love with him and looked forward to our life together, but aware he had some issues with same-sex attraction. I didn't really understand what it meant. I didn't know it couldn't change or he wouldn't be attracted to women as well as men. We were both virgins, and, with my limited knowledge about sex, I assumed that whatever issues he had would be totally resolved once we were intimate. To say I was naïve about sexual matters would be a massive understatement.

We spent the early years of marriage going to college and trying to make the best of our marriage. I really loved him and felt that it was returned; however, I did have sexual disappointments early on. I wanted to be intimate much more often than he and felt rejected and sad many times. But neither of us ever saw that problem as a reason to break up the marriage. We'd made a commitment and would stick to is no matter what. I understood that everyone had their cross to carry in life and this was ours. I also had the kind of faith that led me to believe he'd be healed by Christ and our lives would be better than ever. We were so conservative, and his parents (who knew he was gay and encouraged him to marry me anyway) made sure he knew there were no other options.

In our culture, nothing was more important than having children and creating a family. Our mothers each had eight children, and we enjoyed being part of a big family. So, after a year or so of college, we started trying to have children. This was a bittersweet time. We were much more intimate than before because we were trying to conceive; and so, I was more content in the marriage. Even SK admitted he thought it was really good for him. Unfortunately, infertility was a problem for us, and we were never able to conceive. SK thought he was being punished by God for his same-sex attraction. After five years of trying, we gave up and ended up adopting 3 children, 2 boys and a girl.

We were thrilled to be parents when our first child came along in 1995, one of the happiest years of my life. We settled into a busy time of raising children and moving with my husband's job a lot.

In 2003, we left the Mormon Church. We had both accepted the fact that he was just plain gay, born this way and not suffering from some sin of same-sex attraction. But we convinced ourselves that our children and friendship were enough to sustain our marriage and continued on in a very sexually unfulfilling marriage, although we did continue to have great conversations and lots of laughter. There were huge disappointments for both of us, but life was not all bad.

By 2007, Thanksgiving Eve, SK dropped the bombshell that began to unravel it all. He'd fallen in love with a man at work and was actively involved in a relationship with him. I was totally in shock. I had not suspected at all that there was anything going on. He was always where he was supposed to be. He was a kind and supportive husband and involved father.

The holidays were a nightmare. I was barely able to keep it together to have a nice Christmas for the children, and there was absolutely no joy in it for me. Every ornament I put on the tree felt like a brick so heavy I could barely get it from the box to place it on a branch. I was constantly in the shower because I didn't want the children to see me cry.

By the end of January, I still hadn't spoken to any friends or family about what was going on. I was a train wreck and in the most emotional pain of my life. That's when I went online and found the Straight Spouse Network and heard about Amity for the first time. I was told about an online support group for straight spouses and joined. That was the most miraculous and supportive thing I did for myself through the whole process. I'd sit and read other stories of straight spouses, with tears running down my face for hours. I couldn't believe how freeing it was to connect with other men and women in my shoes.

For SK, the relationship with the man at work did not last; but it was the first serious gay relationship he'd ever experienced, and its ending sent him into a massive depression. I worried he'd commit suicide. Even though I was angry with him, I wasn't prepared to parent my three children alone. I knew the marriage was over but didn't know how to proceed. One night, he didn't come home until 10 the next morning, and I couldn't reach him on his cell. I was terrified he'd killed himself. He had never stayed out all night in nearly 20 years of married life. He told me he got drunk, passed out, and fell asleep at some guy's house. We never drank, and he was very hung over. Luckily, that was a rude awakening for him, and he started to pull out of the depression.

Since we left Mormonism, we started to attend a church that was gay friendly. So, the idea that he may not be going to hell after all and didn't have to suppress who he really was paved the way for him to embrace the idea that he could live as a gay man. Despite everything, I agree. I just wish it didn't have to have caused me so much pain. If anyone could change themselves for gay to str8, he would have done it. He tried so hard to be married and be faithful and a number of times, sobbed, saying, "I'd do anything to make myself straight. I hate myself. I hate I'm gay."

At the time it all blew up, my children were 7, 10, and 12, the boys just entering adolescence. It's been some very rocky years with parenting, and I don't know how much would have happened anyway. Teen years are just plain hard for everyone. One of my children also has some mental health issues, and we've been dealing with that throughout this whole process. I am often overwhelmed with parenting issues and feel like I'm not doing a very good job.

SK and I had one very rocky year where communication was extremely difficult. Most conversations ended up being over email for a while. I felt completely abandoned. I knew he wanted to remain a good father, but he was in such a painful emotional place, he could barely see through it all. One day, I was so angry at him for something he hadn't done for the children, we ended up in a yelling match. He said, "Why are you so mad? I always put you first. I do everything you want me to do."

My response was something like "Don't put me first. I'm a grownup. I can take care of myself. Put the kids first. They're just children."

As hard as everything was, my greatest fear was being left to parent alone. That is where I needed the most help. It also made me crazy to think of doing this to my children. I had purposefully gone out of my way to adopt these children and bring them into my family. You never do that with the intention that you'll bring them into a broken family.

How deeply naïve and in denial I was for most of my life that I really never thought this gay problem would impact our marriage and family! I clearly believed that our family unit was strong enough to bring 3 little children into it and give them the best possible home. I was absolutely heartbroken that this family was falling apart for my children. They did not deserve this. The pain of this was a heavy burden. I knew we had disappointed our Mormon family deeply when we left the church, and they felt we weren't raising our children the right way. I had only my intuition and sense of right and wrong to rely on. I couldn't continue to raise them in a way I didn't believe. But, to completely break the family apart added an incredible level of guilt and grief to the painful burden I already carried.

My oldest son was 12 when his father told him he was gay. I thought we'd tell the children together. Initially I was upset, then a little relived. My son didn't seem that affected by it at the time, but he had a rough freshman year. We'd sold the house, and I moved into an apartment with the kids for a year. The move was hard on him. He'd changed schools and got involved with friends who were not the best for him. That happens to a lot of children in stable families too, right? I have no idea what things were related to our family dynamics changing and what he'd have experienced as a teenager anyway. He is my outgoing child, and he tells all his friends his dad is gay. He doesn't seem to have any problems with it at the moment. He cracks gay jokes all the time, and he and his dad laugh together at them. He seems to be comfortable with it all and enjoys being part of something unconventional and different.

My second son was 10 when it happened and oblivious. About six months after it began, SK and I sat him down to have the conversation. He was clearly in shock and cried. Later on that night, he went around the house saying things like "Some people thought Abe Lincoln was gay." He tried to process it, but it took a long time since he was battling his own emotional demons. One night after we moved into the apartment, he started screaming at me, "Why can't we all live together? Why can't Dad live with us? I just want us all to be together." That was another heartbreaking moment that I thought would truly rip me apart. He has made a lot of progress dealing with his father being gay. He never told his friends and made it clear that if it wasn't for his dad, he'd be completely against anything gay and gay rights. Despite that, he has an amazingly close relationship with his father. He also has a wonderful relationship with his father's partner, who's been in the picture nearly 3 years.

To his credit, the partner has been wonderful to my children, nothing but supportive. He has been helpful many times as we've been dealing with my son's mental health issues. On a number of occasions when he was going through a difficult time, the boyfriend picked him up and they'd spend quality time together, like going to a movie.

My daughter was 7 and didn't know what was going on until we moved. The impact of leaving the house and neighborhood was probably the hardest on her. With her, the conversation happened gradually. She's growing up knowing her father is gay. The other day after her father took her clothes shopping for school, she said to me, "And this is why I like having a gay dad. He's good with clothes."

We were good co-parents. We made it through the first year with verbal communication painful for both of us. The second year, we began to communicate better but mostly about issues regarding the children. The third year, things became more relaxed. We have moved back into an easy friendship. We talk a lot about things beyond parenting. We've gone to the theater a couple of times together. I think we will always be close friends. Friendship, conversation, and laughter were always our strong suit and made a lot of great memories from our marriage. I just needed the time to distance myself and separate from thinking of him as the man I'd spend the rest of my life with. For a while, the grief was too heavy to lay aside for friendship.

In the year following our breakup, I met and fell in love with a wonderful straight man in my support group. We began a long-distance relationship that completely opened my eyes to what a sexual relationship between a man and a woman is really about. I literally had no idea what I'd been missing. In some ways, I feel like I had sex for the first time when I was 42-years old. It was truly one of the most healing experiences I had as I tried to navigate the new terrain of my life, and it helped create a distance from the trauma of my marriage ending. Both of us were dealing with a strong sense of rejection from our marriages' ending, and we were able to help mend the broken pieces of our hearts together. Ultimately, the distance and money proved to be too much to keep the relationship going, but I still consider him a close friend and hold him in a very special place in my heart. Since then, I have dated off and on and had a couple of short-lived relationships, but nothing has clicked in the relationship department. It's frustrating to be single at 45, definitely not where I expected to be at this age with teenage children. Sometimes, I feel like I have too much on my plate to be involved in a relationship. I can only spread my energy so thin, so I take a break from the dating game. Then, after a while, I end up right back in it again. The pull to be with a partner is strong and maybe stronger for us straight spouses. Me, I need to make up for years lost.

Allen...

First, you should know I'm an engineer and look at things with a "This won't work" skeptical eye. People should not be looked upon like that, but I will, when pushed.

Eight years ago, I found out my wife was lesbian. We'd been having email problems and, on checking, I found a huge (1600+) trove of Yahoo emails, some on my daughter's computer. I suspected these were between my wife and her professor friend, so I didn't pry. But there were so many, and why did she go to the trouble of Yahoo accounts when she had good normal email access? So, I snooped. Pretty quickly, I realized this wasn't normal gal chatter; they were lovers in a physical relationship. Mentioning sex stuff like a hotel rendezvous was a clue.

I remember the feeling, standing in my study when I realized it – swimming headache, not able to stand. So I went to lie down. I must have crashed and fallen asleep, the last decent sleep I was to have for a while. It was a good thing she was away at a high school reunion and the kids were visiting their mother.

In the mourning [sic], the confused obsessing started. Like a cough, I couldn't stop thinking, "WHY? WHY? WHY?" Over the weekend, my thoughts gaggled up into three insoluble areas: 1) Why the H3ll did she date men? Wouldn't it be gross? When I met her, she was living in a big city, working for a big corp and a gay boss. An extremely intelligent and independent woman, with family far away and parents deceased, she could have lived authentically as an honest lesbian instead of trying to pass. Far easier for her than most GLBT persons; 2) Why did she cheat on me? She'd argued at length that infidelity was immoral and outrageous, how matricide was understandable if not excusable. Now here she was, the "perp"; and 3) How could she be trusted in the future? Some of her emails mentioned divorcing me, and there wasn't a kind word about me, even when her lover spoke kindly of her own lesbian partner of nineteen years.

It became painfully clear that these questions had no answers. Unknowable is an answer, enough to act upon. The good news was I didn't need to confront her and worry about lies or amorous manipulation. The emails and other paper trails had all the answers needed with fewer, more predictable lies. I was not going to hang around waiting for the axe to fall, nor extort some kind of contrition, a hidden axe. I could not be intimate with her, knowing her preferences were elsewhere. That would be either rape or patronizing a prostitute, and I will not abase myself. Nor would I live without intimacy, and taking a mistress was unacceptable. How could I put a woman I love in second place?

So divorce it was. If she was truly sorry (how could I know?), it could be withdrawn. I was afraid of the confrontation because she had no hesitation using harsh words and occasionally resorted to non-lethal physical abuse (kicking, scratching). But the storm came and, with precautions, eventually passed without damage.

The kids had to be told. They took the news with barely disguised glee. My son (12) had complained of his stepmom's discipline, which I'd explained was her right even if I'd do something different. My daughter (11) smugly said she'd suspected, but I knew she would miss her stepmom in ways she could not know. Not the best reactions, but the best expected.

My soon-to-be-ex stormed, livid. This puzzled me until I read "It is human nature to hate those we have wronged. [Tacitus]," written below the signature of a straight spouse's email message. My soon-to-be-ex also spat hateful things, notably, "It could just as easily have been with a man!" Ouch, until I realized she was wrong in an unexpected direction: her affair would have been much easier with a man -- more opportunity (candidates), more acceptance, less disruption, and much less career risk. She went to some trouble, so lesbianism must have been unusually compelling.

Coping was a separate matter. (Hey, I'm male and I compartmentalize. Live with it.) One cornerstone was scientific findings that sexual orientation (more in men, but sometimes in women) is set at birth (a combination of genes activated during gestation); and, although behaviors could vary, preferences were fixed. Lord knows, many have tried and failed miserably except for a few "true" bisexuals, who could squelch one side because the other was fulfilled.

The Gay Thing was really weird, and I was a little afraid of becoming unjustifiably biased, homophobic. I knew I needed help working this out and most probably not from ordinary straight people. (My mother blames my shoes! – insufficiently dressy shoes meant I had to "settle" for a lesbian.) So I talked with a Diversity person at work, who recommended PFLAG. I went a couple of times, but they were focused differently and mentioned the local straight spouse support group – more my speed, a group of wives and husbands, (mostly "ex"), who had been similarly deceived. I went weekly at first and continue to visit occasionally.

I felt worst just after the divorce was finalized. Not because I regretted anything, but because the fight adrenalin was gone. I could no longer be task-anchored and had to resolve stuff. The biggest learning amid the pain (and realizing we all hurt in different ways) was that the problem was not homosexuality, but D_E_C_E_I_T. There were a few gay-straight couples that managed to stay together, and the common thread was respect and trust, maybe some willful ignorance, but no deceit.

The deceit is unusually nasty because not only did I lose the future (which everyone in a breakup does) but I also lost a big chunk of my past. I cannot think back on any “happier times” without wondering what part her latent lesbianism played. So, off limits.

On the other hand, The Gay Thing is oddly impersonal. Nothing I did or didn’t do made her gay. She already was when she met me. I fell in love, but she chose me for rational reasons.

I suffered not for my failings, but for my qualities. Hey, how many guys could satisfy a lesbian for six seconds, let alone six years?

Support outside straight spouses is sporadic. Nobody knows what to do, and many tip-toe around the gay issue. My gay friends had no problem: this was deceit, pure and simple. All of them had suffered deceit and were quite sympathetic. Emotional support for men is MIA in general. Maybe chicken-and-the-egg, but emotion in men is feared or mocked and only anger (not really an emotion, but a style of expression) is remotely acceptable. I can’t change that. I can only be me and do not need to accept all of society’s straight jackets.

Now, I’ve been very happily remarried for six years. It’s wonderful to love fully (part of self-expression) and be loved back. This is an important lesson for my kids: Finding someone to love you back won’t happen unless you look for it.

One thing still bugs me: those sanctimonious (usually religious) homophobes. GLBT people have never hurt them, yet they attack them. I have been hurt, yet can clearly see the issue is not homosexuality, rather the deceit these GLBT-bashers witlessly encourage.

Leslie…

Where do I begin? This story began so long ago. I'll start about 20 years back.

My ex-spouse and I met while working as paramedics. We were each dating other people and were just friends. As will happen after break-ups, we started dating and, after about two years, we were engaged. I should have known better. As early as six months prior to the wedding, I was ducking flying objects and crying because I was called every horrible name in every conceivable combination. Our friends threw us a couple's wedding shower, some call it a "Jack and Jill." He walked out because he was mad at me for not taking his side in an argument he had with a groomsman. He threw our puppy down a flight of stairs because it chewed "my" shoe! That's just a token accounting.

Sex, initially, was ok mechanically. But as time wore on and he became more abusive, the sex was less about me and more about his need to get off. I could have been a blow up doll or a tree, and it got to the point where I was no longer interested.

We lived in his childhood home while gathering money to buy our own house. In about two years, having just about worn out our welcome at his mom's place, we saved enough for a down payment; so house hunting took place. We bought a 3-bedroom, 1 ½-bath, on lots of land.

Several years later during my first pregnancy, I experienced my first lengthy stay at home. I'm a firefighter, and there are no light duty assignments. I stayed busy, like painting bedrooms, cleaning closets, and moving furniture. While I did try to get a temporary part time job, no one would hire me because I wasn't staying.

My husband played on my guilt about not having a "job," though I had saved and taken out a plan that paid me partial salary during my leave. In his eyes, I was a loser, a freeloader, and a bitch for taking all of his money. I kept looking at myself and trying to figure out why I made him so mad. The harder I tried, the madder he seemed to get. I quit trying to figure out that pretzel logic. We were the typical American family with the mortgage and white picket fence, right? We had our first child and those on the outside would have said we were a lovely family. On the inside, things were not so rosy. I should have known better. I stood up for myself and spoke my mind, back then. Three years and three children later, nothing changed.

There were a few times I was hoping for better, like when I miscarried our fourth child. Devastated, I planned the D & C. He took me to the outpatient surgery center. I remember crying as I went under anesthesia and crying, coming out. When we arrived home, he got out of the car and relieved his mother of child care duties for our other three young children. Once his mother was out of sight, it was a tirade of name-calling and screaming all in the name of "I took too long in surgery." I was tired, in pain, and bleeding. I was also depressed, having just lost a child. After he was done, he turned and walked out for the rest of the day and night.

Over the next two years, we had our last two children. By our fifth and last child, I was much quieter and much more careful. When yelled at, I just stood there and waited for him to leave. I knew I was on my own before, during, and after delivery. While on maternity leave, I had the most stunning revelation of my life. I discovered my autistic son, 6 at the time, viewing gay porn on the family computer! Sending him to another room to play, I found what was horrifying: hundreds of videos; gay, hemale/shemale, everything but straight porn.

I confronted my husband that night. He lied and said they just popped up out of nowhere. I wasn't buying it. Strangely enough, he finally admitted that he was a transvestite and had been since he was about twelve. In the months following my discovery, I joined a support group, SSN or Straight Spouse Network. It was started by Amity Buxton. The group was a lifeboat for me. I never joined anything, but I was desperate and had nowhere to turn. I found hope in other stories and a sense of not being alone in this horror show.

In the months that followed, I found evidence of my husband's "true" self: dresses, clothes, makeup, jewelry, wigs, and shoes with little pointed toes. Most horrifying and what brought the whole mess front and center for me, although you may think there were huge flags waving all along, was when I discovered two smallish boxes in his closet. When I opened them, they revealed two boobs! Yes, you read that correctly: boobs. They were all pink and perky, sitting there in their specially molded cup holders! In that moment of discovery, I knew my marriage was really over. I was sadly aware that my dream of having a huge family was crushed, along with so many other dreams. It may seem a little strange, but I've always wanted to live off the land and have a family that worked together, lived together, and played together. I had to live with the reality that everything I ever wanted was forever crushed and decided that I could just try to live together with this person I'm supposed to call my husband as peacefully as possible until the kids were older and then move on. He had different plans.

He filed for divorce exactly one year after I had been back to work full time. Our youngest child was three. He refused to move out until the judge ordered it. He tried to bully me into a quick divorce, giving him the kids half the time, me taking all the debt and no child support or alimony, no share in his savings, stocks, or pension. I refused. He threatened to bury me under court debt and did. He turned issues which could have been settled quickly into a 5-day trial.

Two years ago, the divorce was final, and life as we know it is very different.

He keeps his "girly-girl" stuff locked in a closet in my boys' bedroom at his house. My eldest daughter is a mess, many days. She is the one he loves to hate, and then loves, and then hates again. He has learned to buy his children's love and affections as he cannot give them emotionally what they need. I hope someday he learns. I have learned to accept what I cannot change and hope I have gained the wisdom to know the difference.

I guess I haven't really lost total sight of my dream as I live for my children. We go everywhere and do everything as a family. My time is my gift to them. They are learning to be responsible little people, even though it is an uphill battle. I love them all more than anything in my world.

I've discovered, post divorce, some very carefully hidden family secrets like the abuse he and his family suffered at the hands of his alcoholic father! In all our years married, this never made its way to my ears. I heard what a great guy his father was and how he overcame alcoholism. I heard how his father was patient and kind, though I clearly remember a few slips during family visits that scared me. As they say…"De-Nile" is a deep, long river.

I have also discovered how typical it is for married transvestites to be so angry. This isn't scientific research. It's just observations from a few counselors and mediators who have had to deal with many couples with a "tranny" in the mix.

As for me? I am working on my own self image. I'm learning to become as comfortable with my body as I have become with me – meaning my mind, my personality, and my sense of humor. What did he do for me? Was there a silver lining? Well, I have come to recognize that he did me a favor. CDWB or Cross Dressing Wonder boy, as he has been dubbed by another straight, unintentionally gave me my freedom. I have the chance to breathe freely and just live. I now can take a look at my life and try to fix in me whatever it was that allowed me to tolerate his abuse. I'm always finding ways to keep my children from abusing or being abused. I have the freedom to really live my life in relative peace. That freedom is the one true gift he's given me.

Ben…

In 1986, I married my best friend and the person I was to grown old with, the woman I had my children by, with whom I shared my innermost being, and whom I thought I knew better than anyone. Little did I know that I did not know anything.

Summer 2000 went on as summers did, me working and my wife with time off, since she drove a school bus. It was the perfect job because she could be there for the kids. This summer, however, things were amiss, with no reason to explain it, I told myself. We were different....no, she was different. She was spending an outrageous amount of time on the computer. I thought she was instant messaging friends and shopping. She was coming to bed later and later. It was strange, but no biggie. Off for the summer, she doesn't need to get to bed when I do.

One day out of the blue, she mentioned she'd found a friend online who had a lot in common with her and three kids of her own.

"O.K.," I said. "That's cool."

Thus, she and her newfound friend were hanging out, going out, and giving a grand ol' girls' time. (How dumb and foolish I feel now.)

One night, we planned to get together with friends from church. I'm Catholic, she was not, but we were all friends. We were to meet for dinner at a local restaurant/bar that had a little band and then hang out. My wife said she'd meet me there. She was the last to show up with "the friend," figuring no one would mind and why would they, if, of course, they were as naïve as I.

Things have a funny way of working out. I was not feeling well and told my wife after dinner that I thought "we" should go home. She told me to go on home as she was staying. Something in my mind raised a flag. But I went home, lay down, and fell asleep. I woke up about 2:00 AM. Since my wife wasn't home and it was unlike her to be out that late, not to mention she wasn't answering her cell, I feared something had happened.

I jumped into the car and drove back to the restaurant just as they were closing. One of the guys in the band was an acquaintance, and I asked him if he'd seen my wife. He went silent and said he needed to tell me something: MY WIFE, THE MOTHER OF MY CHILDREN, in front of our church friends, had seductively danced, and made out with, and carried on with her "friend." I was sick and stunned. Since I didn't know what to do, I went home and waited. She showed up about 3:00 AM.

When I asked her what the hell was going on and said I'd spoken with the guy in the band, she broke down and told me she was drunk and confused, the friend made a move on her, and she didn't know what to do. I asked what else took place, and she swore no more than the kissing. I threw her pillow and blanket out of our bedroom, locked myself in, and went to sleep.

The next morning, I thought long and hard about my vows and the kids and everything we'd been through and decided not to throw away fourteen years due to a mistake. I told her how I felt and that we would work through this. "But," I said, "there is no way that you are ever to see or talk to that 'friend' ever again."

She agreed. As days went on, she tried negotiating various ways of allowing contact with her friend, via email or instant message, and I said no way. If she valued our marriage, she would honor this and not bring it up again. Her next step was to get nasty, telling me I had no right to tell her who she could and could not see. I explained that, when she broke the marital bond of trust, I was given that right. "Either you want to be married to me or you want to get with her, but you cannot have it both ways. If you want the latter, pack your bags and leave, but understand that, once you walk out that door, you will never come back."

One September 1, 2000, she did just that. With no warning or chance to explain to our kids, she packed her bags, told them she was leaving, and asked them to do the same. They were shocked and stunned and crying. They refused to go with her (and for that I will be eternally grateful), and off she went. When the screen door shut, our lives had just changed forever.

My wife died that day. The person I married, caring and thoughtful, who loved our kids, was no longer here. Her face and body were evident, but all shards of that woman were gone. She became erratic and moody with severe emotional swings, and her parental sense was completely gone. She thought only of herself and her new-found life as a lesbian. Our kids had to take it or leave it. Their first weekend with her, she took them to the now girlfriend's house, where they watched their mother have a physical relationship with this woman and go to bed with her, the door left open.

I filed for divorce, which began a four-year battle, in which she told the neighbors she left because I beat her. She called the police and told them the same thing. The transformation was like nothing I've ever witnessed. She accused me of a gay relationship when I invited a man and his two kids to live with us after their home burned down and they had no place to live. She broke into the family home several times by kicking in the door, tried opening credit cards in my name so she could use them, and caused irreparable harm to both kids. My daughter has not spoken to her mother in over six years. My son sees her once a week for two hours.

I retained custody of both kids -- unheard of in my conservative county where mothers are almost always granted custody -- and got to keep the house. Now I am a 44-year-old single dad of two teenagers. While I wouldn't trade this for anything, I am angered that I was put in this position to look the fool while she walked away, leaving me not only to pick up the pieces, but also to mend them and heal our children, try to be a mother figure in some form, and wonder what will become of my life now. I do not communicate with her unless it's necessary and related to the kids and only through email.

I will never forgive her for what she did to me, but mostly what she did to two wonderful kids who deserve none of this.

SS…

After several long talks, we agreed we'd work on the marriage together, and she joined a bisexual web site. At first, it seemed we might be able to make it work. She shared her feelings and was open about what she wanted. We started talking about polyamory and swinging and any other option. We briefly tried swinging in the summer of 2006: one encounter with another couple that also included a bisexual woman. It was fairly tame, but she enjoyed it. A couple weeks later, she said that swinging wasn't for her and she wanted an intimate relationship with a woman. At this point, she was still telling me she was bisexual and intimacy between us had not changed, so I continued to believe her. (I think she still believed it too, but I'm not sure.) Reluctantly, I agreed that she find a happily married bisexual woman and that our relationship remain obviously primary.

By October of last year, she'd met someone online and they started dating. It started slowly, and, according to her, the dates were awkward. In December, they had their first intimate experience. Immediately, my wife started sharing less than everything about her relationship with this woman. Within two months, she began having major problems being with me as she was spending more and more time with her girlfriend. She also started lying about things they did together. By March, I told her I could no longer support her relationship and that, unless we were obviously primary, I wanted her to stop seeing this woman.

For months, she went back and forth between telling me she wasn't sure she could be with me or thought we'd be OK and work this out. This first limbo stage, I was falling apart and becoming severely depressed and she could see all of this yet did not stop. For a few months, we still had fun when we were together. Our sex life continued into early summer, but it was awkward at best and infrequent. We also started therapy together.

In July, I went backpacking with a couple of long-time friends I don't see often because we live far apart. During the trip, I actually started to feel like a somewhat normal person again. The first time in five months, I realized how miserable her actions were making me and that I couldn't live like this any longer. When I got home, I told her that her relationship with this woman was over or we were getting a divorce as soon as possible. She got angry and withdrew from me and her girlfriend.

At that point, I had a near mental breakdown one night (probably had more, but this one was really bad). When it ended, I concluded the best thing to do was to accept who she was. I told her that I accepted her being a lesbian and wanted to stay friends and work out the best arrangements for the kids' sake. We both cried a ton, and, for the first time in months, I could tell she still cared about me and our relationship. She did break it off with her girlfriend, but not before they had one more night together. (Nice, huh!)

She didn't make a clean break. It was more like a temporary break while she decided what to do about us. She's still in the same place although her girlfriend has moved on. She thinks she's a lesbian yet not sure she is ready to break up the family because of it. This is the second limbo stage. I feel depression trying to make a strong comeback.

In September, she decided we should consider a trial separation. We live in the same house but sleep in separate beds. We spend time as a family, but there's no intimacy. She explores her lesbian identity, as far as I know only in non-intimate ways, with a support group and lesbian friends she talks to regularly. She's reading about relationships, divorce, etc. She just put a HRC (Human Rights Campaign) bumper sticker on her car.

You may call me a moron for going along with some of this. (I've called myself that many times.) But I thought we were life partners and would support each other no matter what. I guess I was half right. I supported her no matter what, and she took all that support and ran with it. I know she is not the right person for me, and I know I deserve better. But I wish there was some way to keep the family together. Every time I convince myself it's time to move on, I look at my kids and just can't end it. My guess is that my wife is having the same problem.

Francsy…

"You've got to be willing to work through the Pain."

It seems this all happened to someone else. Breaking down 27 years of Dante's Inferno is just surreal.

I live in Kent, England. Ryan and I met in 1982 while he held the priesthood. We married in '84. The weeks before the wedding foreshadowed the entire marriage: insecurity, infidelity, depression, lying, hiding, and deceit. One day, we were walking to church and saw a group of Punk Rocker blokes.

"Would you ever fancy someone like that?" my husband asks. It wasn't quite rhetoric.

I didn't know how to respond. He fell pale and silent. I touched his arm and asked if he was ok. "Was it something I said?"

We held an awkward silence most of the day. He withdrew. Too bad it took me 27 years to find out the cost of that conversation.

That night, lying in his arms, I begged him to talk, knowing something was wrong. "You can trust me. Please be honest with me!"

He told me he'd enjoyed gay love affairs whilst at college in London and still felt attraction to men; but, since joining the church, he'd been celibate. He thought he was bisexual but would never act on it. He promised monogamy and reassured me he wanted me in every conceivable way and was in love with only me. We cried and cuddled and tried desperately to tell ourselves we would be ok. I was a prisoner held captive in an invisible cell. It was solitary confinement. I had no one to talk to. I suffered in silence.

We married. Time and experience has shown us to be extremely naïve. Love doesn't conquer all. It helps a whole lot. But it isn't enough. I learned early on you've got to be wiling to work through the pain.

1985 – Our first anniversary. We had an argument, and he responded with the usual withdraw. He'd been undemonstrative for quite some time. I left him curled up on the sofa feeling sorry for himself. When I got back a few hours later, he was still curled up on the sofa. I asked what was wrong. He said he didn't know. I knew he was lying. I sat down with him and gave him a cuddle, and he just cried for hours.

I know now. He'd been having intense same-sex attractions and was in the middle of an "ah ha" moment, a flashpoint, a breakdown. He realised no matter how good we were, *our* love wasn't enough and something was still missing.

Over the next decade, we worked to appease each other. To be the understanding wife, I incorporated play into our sex life as a kind of compensation. Sounds silly, but the intentions were good. I slowly got used to sex acts that are a huge part of gay life, and yet we still enjoyed "normal" straight sex on every level and permutation. He was giving and thoughtful. My pleasure was his pleasure.

As time went on, our daily lovings dwindled to one a week. He excused away our lack of intimacy as work or money worries. He suffered from ongoing depression and, when our third child was born, regressed miserably. Thus I knew 1997 would be a difficult year. To this point, although he had same-sex attractions, I thought he was faithful. That's what I thought.

He came home very late one night and slept on the sofa. In all our years together, he never slept anywhere but in our bed, so I knew something was very, very wrong. He finally told me he'd been unfaithful once. He'd pulled into a motorway service station and used the loo. A guy was at the urinal, showing him his penis. He said he got rock hard, and the guy noticed. They touched each other and eventually went to the guy's flat and had sex.

We talked, cried, talked, and cried more. He told me how he needed me, wanted me, and would never hurt me again. And I took down all the photos of him, put them in a steel bowl, and set them on fire in the bed! (I just had that quilt mended!)

It turned out he'd kept the guy's number and was trying desperately to figure out how to meet his needs without compromising his promise made to me. It was then he suggested it wouldn't be cheating if we had a threesome. Though I couldn't believe he was suggesting swinging, I gave apprehensive approval. He was so happy -- like an excited little puppy. "Just once," he said, "and, if it doesn't feel right for you, I'll never ask again." It wasn't just once. Whenever he couldn't get satisfaction from his own pursuits or felt insecure or threatened by relationships I'd establish, he'd insist on 3-ways.

One night, he came home with phone numbers copied from a public loo and rang one. Shaking, I thought, "Oh my God. This can't be happening, it just can't." Well it could and did.

As a matter of fact, "it" happened on our 13th wedding anniversary. He'd set up our rendezvous in a nice hotel room for us, and the guy agreed to meet us there. A big part of me felt threatened by m2m sex. Why was it so beautiful to him? Why did he need it so? I thought that, if I could see it, I'd understand.

In reality, it was embarrassing. As soon as they climaxed, I went to the bathroom to wipe it all away. I came back out to find them sitting on the bed. Ryan had his arm round the guy, appearing to console our new acquaintance; and the guy had his head in his hands, saying he was sorry but couldn't stay, needed to go. Coming out of my numbness, I felt sorry for them both.

The next morning, I felt like shit. "Dirty" Isn't the right word; "used" is closer. I was a mummy of three kids, 10, 8, and 2, and couldn't get the two scenarios to match up. I didn't like myself and asked Ryan to let me off. I couldn't do it anymore, at least not while the kids were so young. He tried to talk me round but gave up pretty quick. He said he was sorry he'd put me through that and would try to understand. I asked him to let me know if the feelings were building up again, and we could see how we felt then. He gave me his promise.

All he did was to go back into the closet. Years later, I got the full story. He'd hardly ever been faithful. The toilets on London Bridge train station are a favorite haunt for many closeted men – which explained all those trains he missed.

By Christmas 2001, two moves took place: we moved deeper into Kent and Ryan moved deeper in the closet. Our eldest son was the victim of gang violence. No arrests were made because a local crime family was involved and people were scared to testify; so we had to move. Ryan was reluctant and sulked. I never understood that as it only added 20 minutes to the overall journey to work and gave him lots more flexibility. Now I understand: he'd be away from London Bridge Station, his regular "quick fix." It took three years more for him to really talk about his romps, and he admitted speaking with other bi married men in a support group. He hadn't wanted to feel like a monster all alone with his feelings.

Knowing he was sexually active with men, I insisted we have synchronized testing to be safe, and that became a part of my "normal" life. One good by-product of this was discovering I am naturally low in HEPb antibodies, and, while with Ryan, needed regular double booster shots. In reality, I became isolated. I shielded his secret and lived his lies. We never told anyone, not even family.

You'd think there were flags or gut instincts to run. Denial protects us. The real turning point was New Year's Day, 2006. I woke up from a nap on the sofa, wondering where he was, and found him at his computer. When I walked up behind him to give him a cuddle, he froze, and I saw a naked man on the monitor screen. "Who's that?"

He told me it was his brother-in-law, and I pushed him hard to confess, reminding him I'm not stupid, nor blind. "Who is it?" I repeated, angrily.

All he admitted was talking to a guy on the site of the bi married men's group where he goes to talk about his feelings. I was so enraged, things got physical. I had bruises on my arms for weeks where he had held up his arms to defend himself.

In the ensuing eight months, after a miserable attempted holiday to Spain, I broke through the password he'd set on our family computer and somehow opened everything. My heart pounding, I couldn't stop opening site after site. I saw it all:

every MSN chat, video, exchanged pictures, and emails going back years. I discovered he was into group gay sex in saunas and the local woods. I found out he'd had a boyfriend for ten months and was very much in love with another bi married man. He'd even taken our son Brian on a meet up. The chats with hundreds of men were raw and graphic. He'd even sent pictures of me to bi men who hoped to have both of us. He'd sent intimate shots of himself at every angle and videos of masturbation.

I phoned him and told him something had come up and he had to come home now. When he got home, I told him what I'd found. He said I'd misunderstood; he hadn't done anything. I can't believe how calm I was. I told him, "I'm not asking. I'm TELLING you I know everything. Please find some respect in yourself to give me the honesty I've been asking for all these years."

It took about an hour, but then he just slumped and gave it all up. He said he would go. It was only then that I started shouting. "How dare you make this fucking mess then think you just can walk away and leave me to sort it out! No fucking way!" I demanded he stay and help me sort it out. Coming clean and being accountable were the last stones left unturned. If he could put that much effort into his gay life, he could put as much into us or clearing up the mess.

I was dealing with the shock of betrayal, his double life, and his infidelity, *not that he was gay.* He agreed to an open marriage, knowing that we both had needs that weren't met. In my mind, I keep going back to our failed summer holiday in Spain. I asked him, "If you had to do it all over again, would you marry me?"

"No," he said, "it's too painful to be married to me."

I still can't remove that double-edged dagger from my heart.

We joined HUGS and that gave him a confidence boost to assume his gay identity. It was the beginning of the coming-out process for him. For the next eighteen months, we went though our open and honest phase in which he felt open enough to tell me everything, more than I wanted to know. It was a post discovery "honeymoon." We bonked for England and felt much closer. He told me he couldn't turn back the clock and needed his m2m, but he'd always need me, too. We felt that making the choice to have an open marriage was the right one for us.

So he set out on his journey to find his special bud, a hunt that grew obsessive. He started an emotional affair with another HUGster, who bailed on him, although his ex-wife and I remained close. I began to look for my special friend, as it was intensely lonely being in the same room with Ryan. I'd never enjoyed his company and had started making more platonic friends, male and female. What I really wanted was to feel what it's like to be with a straight man. I needed to know if a straight man and I would have our unique energy in the same way that gay men say they do. I found it easier to make male friends. Some became lovers. I never lied or hid it, and Ryan would even have their telephone numbers for safety and in case of emergency. I met some lovely men over the years, many still long term special friends. Some lovers lasted for two to three years, some for months.

Ryan had a problem that I wasn't a "fuck and go gal." He felt threatened by my ability to form meaningful relationships apart from him and became jealous that men liked ME, not just my body or what I could do for them. He hated he wasn't the centre of the universe. When he opened our marriage, he thought he'd be the one to be fulfilled. He was still lonely, not having the life he envisioned, and demanded I choose them or him. When I eventually chose them, he told me I had never loved him, that I was a lousy wife, and that he would learn to hate me and to stop loving me. Our tensions were cyclical.

Whilst all this was going on, Ryan wanted to pursue a lifelong dream and emigrate to Canada. He ended up admitting that it was because he was in love with his bi married lover and how hard it was to find someone who wanted HIM not just his giant cock. We never made it to Canada. Sadly, dreams die, hopes die, and my father, who had a stroke 12 years before, passed away-- the trigger for Ryan to finally let go of any restraints and indulge his appetites openly.

By March 2008, his hunt was less fruitful, and he began to pressure me to do 3-ways again. I said no. I told him I'd already been down that road and he had rubbished it, saying it wasn't fulfilling. He told me I was being a selfish bitch for denying him that. My refusal to give in and my ability to stand my ground were the beginning of the end.

Ryan never felt the emotional price tag of my loneliness: the isolation. I had to illustrate it for him and mirrored his behavior to drive home the point. I stopped considering his feelings and acknowledging him and put myself first. I was glad to allow him to experience the shoe on the other foot. When he realized that I was playing my own version of his psychological games, he demanded I stop and put him first. He proclaimed he was man enough for me sexually and, if I needed company for intimacy, I should find a lesbian!

He didn't understand my needs, and I had no desire any longer to help him understand.

I told him no and I would continue with my social pursuits. I also offered that if I knew a shortcut through the pain of sharing, I'd do what I could. It's an awful pain to grow through, but there's no shortcut.

By Christmas, everyone in the family knew. We were in separate rooms and in desperate need of separate lives. My personal line in the sand was when he broke his honesty and safety commitment he'd made to our "new open marriage" and failed us. His behavior didn't say, "I value you, our family, what we have, what you do for me," but rather that he couldn't get past what he DIDN'T have: a man who wanted HIM, all of him. His whole focus on and misery about that eclipsed any happiness he should have felt with his home life and me. He always called me the love of his life, his soul mate. But, in the end, he didn't value that. As he aged, he needed men more than he thought he needed me.

It was obvious that living together, separated under one roof, was unworkable. We had a terrible fight. I locked myself into my bedroom and called the police who came immediately. It was an emotionally violent explosion. They told me it was abuse and marital rape, and they made him leave.

I did allow him back.

But, by that January, 25 years into our marriage, I was finally ready for a trial separation. He refused. In August, I took my youngest, Brian, and visited another straight wife in Holland for a few days to get my thoughts settled. When I was away, Ryan struck up an online friendship with a young 32-year-old and, without telling anyone where he was going, went off for a long weekend, using my car. When my son and I returned to England and didn't find the car, I texted him to say the car was stolen. He texted back, 30 min later, to tell me where he was and that he'd be late picking us up. The text began. "I know this will sound off the wall but..."

I cried most of the way home because I knew that a trial separation was not enough and he couldn't break the bad old habits and give me honesty and safety. We were over. By now, we had only one agreement left in place: play safely. He'd broken the never-go-off-anywhere- without- letting-someone-know rule. Luckily, Brian knew about his dad. He gave me some cuddles and, at one point, whispered, "He'll never change, Mum. It's not worth it. I'm ok if you want to heave him. We'll manage!"

We waited two and a half hours at the terminal and were exhausted when Ryan finally turned up, completely unaware of how it had made us feel to be made to wait. I waited till the following morning to ask him how it had happened. He gave me a song and dance. I didn't buy it. I asked for divorce.

He begged for our marriage, saying he was in a "straight" phase, needed me, and would rather die than live without me. Eventually, he agreed to go to the doctor and was referred for psychosexual therapy. He was put on strong anti-depressants and sleeping tablets, which the doctor asked me to hold and administer because of his suicidal threats. He sent me long texts, alternating between loving and sensual to threats and anger, saying he hoped no one would ever love me enough or touch me the way I needed to be touched or that he wished that nobody would ever want me as much as he does. Then he'd revert to pleas of love and commitment.

At the end, I told him I hoped his friendship with Nicky would grow into something special and worth breaking our rules for. I was throwing in the towel. I quit. It was over. It was over for Nicky, too. He died of Aids in January 2010.

At the divorce, Ryan cried, and I cried. He tears were for what he had lost and how he has suffered. For me, it was a sad day and also a day of increased understandings.

The divorce over, we are selling our final asset, the house. I often think back how this monster literally "fed" on me. It's called "emotional vampirism." Ryan has never understood how hard this has been for me, how I went way beyond what many women would "put up with," as I tried so hard to give back. I thought he'd been mostly monogamous and what I thought this had cost him. As a way of making it up to him, I cut him huge slack in other areas.

August 2010, Brian found a letter I'd written to his dad when he was just two and a half, in which I poured out all that I felt and what I was trying do to make life easier for him. As I read it, the tears came again. I'd tried so hard for so long. When we met after court, I'd told him, "I never said I don't love you. I will always love you. I just can't be your wife anymore." Not once did he tell me he loved me. This letter underlined why I eventually ran out of steam and could never love him enough to balance the books. His effort had to equal mine, and he found out too late that it never did. He still couldn't give me his unselfish love.

In closing, I think a lot of us are strong and we learn to manage in an unusual situation. It wasn't until I was alone that I realized how much he'd dragged me down. Our husbands lynch off of us and drain our life. Emotional vampirism is rampant. Now, I feel a part of the world again. I can be myself, let my hair down, and, most of all, have genuine friendships. It sounds silly but I'm more me again. I laugh more, tease more, and do more. I have made deeper friendships and have discovered the truth to what a very wise straight wife told me when I joined my first support group: "When the pain of staying outweighs the pain of leaving, you'll leave."

Clarence…

Friday night, February 26, she'd gone to the big city hospital 80 miles away to see the sick friend. She called halfway home and said she was tired and was going to stay at the bowling friend's house. So I wondered, but always gave her plenty of freedom, and she always came home -- which she did, Saturday afternoon. I went out to help her carry in groceries, (which she said she'd stop for), and there were none. She said she'd gone to an AA meeting with this new friend that Saturday morning instead. I thought that was a little out of character, as she liked a little drink from time to time and it would be boring for her

The next week, something was different, but I couldn't tell what. I realized afterwards that she hadn't mentioned the bowling friend. (Side note: she'd told me earlier that she was afraid to be friends with this person because this person might "cling on" to her.) Friday, I got up in the morning and fixed her lunch while she got ready for work. She came to give me a kiss before leaving and said, "I'm going to stay in town tonight."

I knew what that meant. I just stared in silence, and she left. I texted her late that night and told her to stay another day so I could sort this out.

Black Sunday (March 7th). I received a text from her about 10:30 AM: "I will be back in a while for stuff. We can talk if you want."

What the hell just happened? How did it come to this? That was it? Just like that?

When she arrived, she told me, "This is something I just have to do." Then she left.

I was devastated. I was trying to understand. I was blaming myself. She called my daughter that day, and my son was told by the daughter. The next day, he got in his truck and drove the 1600 miles in 28 hours to be here to console me. God bless him.

After my son went home, my wife came back with a moving truck and took a bunch of the extras from around the house. A couple we had hung out with helped her. It was hard, but my friend was right: "Better them than some stranger helping her move."

Before she left, she told me, "I will always love you. This was not your fault. You did nothing wrong. There is nothing you could have done. This is hard on me, too."

If that's the case, why does it feel as if I am the only one to pay the penalty?

The last time I saw her was March 27th. She had an old Corvette to get and a few more clothes left in our closet. I thought the friends were going to help her get the car because they offered. She showed up with the new girlfriend. Wow. Salt for the wound. I asked her if she was salting my wound, and she said, "No. This was just easier."

Not for me. My son talked to her later, and she admitted that she did it to show her new girlfriend what she gave up for her. Ouch. At my expense.

Since then, she has her own place. She does not live with the girlfriend, just sleeps there. She says it's too hard on both of us to contact each other. We're supposed to use the same lawyer to make it cheaper. She wants nothing else but is dragging her feet. My life is upside down.

Anger, loneliness, heart ache and confusion, crying, longing were daily problems. Lost 25 pounds since then. Chain-smoking. (I'd almost quit on the Chantix when this happened.) Can't sleep. I have yet to hear my alarm clock before work since this happened. The only good thing was that, after she left, I didn't have a single drink for a week and a half. I thought it would be too easy to crawl into a bottle and hide. Now I just drink in moderation. Just enough to be calm.

Van…

My wife and I were together for 15 years, married for 12. She was my best friend and the love of my life. Sure, we had problems but learned to communicate well and worked through anything that came up. I had two kids from a previous marriage who lived in another state, and, because of a very bad relationship with my ex, I wasn't able to see them. My wife also brought two kids to our marriage. We were very active and decided we didn't want any more kids, so I agreed to have a vasectomy to eliminate the mistake factor. Eventually, my wife's biological clock got the best of her, and she decided she wanted us to have two more kids together, close in age so they could grow up together as best friends. Though I didn't want more kids, I agreed to have a reversal. It was successful. We had two boys, nineteen months apart.

The only nagging problem was the physical part of our relationship. I wanted to be intimate several times a week, where she would have been content with once a month. We talked and even went to counseling. I eventually negotiated a once-a-week schedule.

One day at a party, "the girls" had a bit to drink and got frisky, teasing the guys. My wife was in on the action. A short time after that, she approached me. She explained that she liked the feeling she had during that encounter and had feelings that she needed to explore and understand. She felt she might be Bi and suggested I allow her to bring another woman into our relationship so she could explore these new feelings. She told me that, if I did this for her, it would prove how much I truly loved her. In return, she would show me more love. She suggested it might bring us closer and would enhance our physical relationship. As always, I agreed. I can't think of more than once or twice I ever told her, "NO," and most likely changed that to "Yes" after a period.

In the process of trying to understand her feelings, she discussed them with her counselor, who suggested she speak with another client who might be able to help her understand them. They met for drinks and immediately had a connection. I agreed to allow them a girls night out weekly as long as they remained in public and did not go off alone to do anything intimate. We agreed that, if any intimate contact was to occur, it had to include me. She would not be cheating then, including me in an encounter to explore these new feelings. As time passed, she included her new friend in many other activities and really incorporated her into the family.

As things progressed, I became more and more concerned. While my wife constantly told me how much she loved me, appreciated what I was doing, and would never leave me, she was beginning to include this new woman in everything we did. We rarely had any alone time. I expressed my concern many times, but she always told me how much she loved me, assured me I had nothing to worry about, and she would never leave me.

About six months later, I was invited out of state to my son's graduation. Since I hadn't seen him in ten years, I jumped at the chance to possibly reconnect. I arranged for my other son (also from my first marriage) to join us. I spent several days reconnecting with them and reassuring them that the things they had heard about me were far from reality. I also used the trip to see my dad, who is not in the best of health. I was gone for 5 days. When I returned, my wife asked me to join her at a counseling session. It was then she told me she was not Bi, but Gay, and would be leaving me to start a new life with her Girlfriend. I was her best friend, the best husband, and the best father any woman could ask for ... but she was Gay. Spending time alone with her girlfriend when I was out of town sealed any doubt she had.

I spent the next twenty minutes exploding on her. I recited many of the out of the ordinary things I'd done for her through our relationship and reminded her how, time and time again, she'd promised that I was doing the right thing and she would never leave me. Her only response was that she made that promise and said those things before she knew she was Gay.

I was devastated. I'd just learned that my best friend, the love of my life, the woman I put on a pedestal and never let down, was leaving me. I wanted to die. The next few months were probably the hardest times of my life. She would move "when the time was right." When I came home from work, she and her girlfriend were on the phone. I quickly learned what a panic attack was. I experienced attacks daily as I watched them plan their lives together, as if I was just there to manage the house and kids. She began to spend more nights away than at home but would still not leave. She said it was for the boys; we needed to transition them slow. But, while we transitioned them, I was the one that cared for them every night while she transitioned to her new life. As I managed the flood of emotions, devastation, anger, hurt, fear, the best way to deal with it was to focus on the boys.

The only way I survived emotionally was to find a group called the Straight Spouse Network and, within that organization, an online group formed called Str8s. Every night after I put the boys to bed, I would go online and lean on them for support. I honestly don't know if I would have survived the months of torment without this group of fantastic people that understood what I was going through. They understood because they were all going through it as well. They were there to listen and understand, but never judge how I handled my situation. Even though we were in similar situations (all had a Gay spouse), there were many variations of how it was dealt with.

After about six months, my wife was spending every night with her new partner, but still had not moved out. She had only taken the necessities. It took 11 months before she really moved. We signed a legal separation agreement which laid the ground work for divorce: division of property, custody, and support. The emotional drain continued as she continued to lean on me for emotional support. She continued to tell me she loved me, just not in "that" way, I was her best friend, the only one that "got" her, and she couldn't imagine her life without me in it. She wanted me to remain her best friend and didn't comprehend why I couldn't be. She thought that, since she was gay, I couldn't love her in that way anymore, like I had a switch I could throw and make us just best friends instead of partners.

Her and her new partner began to have problems. They'd fight after a night out. Her partner would throw her out, and she'd call me to get her. She used me and my home as a backup or escape if she needed it. She even came back and stayed in the spare room for a week a couple times. I couldn't bring myself to turn her away, though I knew it was not good for either of us.

Just before she left the last time, we had a long talk. I let her know she could no longer come home. "We'll never be able to truly move on if it continues."

She asked twice since to come back or for me to get her. I was able to make alternative suggestions so it didn't happen.

It's been about one and a half years since this started. I've attempted to connect with other women and am currently in what we call a relationship, with no emotional attachment. I care a lot for her as we've been friends since high school, but I don't love her. Before her, I became close to another woman. We were able to talk and understand each other. She is a wonderful person with a lot to offer the right man, but I was unable to connect beyond a great friendship. I didn't feel that "thing" that leads to love and being partners. At this point, I find myself numb, unable to feel emotionally attached. I enjoy the physical part of the relationship, but even find that difficult at times as I realize it's just physical.

I continue to talk to the straight spouses mailing list and have gone to two gatherings, where many get together from all across the world to help each other through the journey we all share. While the intensity of emotions has diminished, I continue to feel the roller coaster of hurt and despair at times. People outside my straight spouses support group have asked why this is different than just getting a divorce. In reflection, it's because, unlike losing a partner, separating and moving on, there continues to be a bond that isn't broken. My wife still wants to be my best friend and leans on me for support. Unlike a spouse that finds another partner and cuts ties, this drags on longer. There isn't a switch in my head to turn off the care I have for her either. When she is hurting because of her family abandoning her, because of her decision to come out, or when her new partner treats her badly, I feel for her. I can't just stop. It's a process that is different than two people in a marriage that deteriorates to where they decide they can't be together any more. For the straight spouse, this process starts when the Gay spouse comes out. That's harder for someone not living this situation to understand.

Emma…

The Serpent and the File

A serpent in the course of its wanderings came into a blacksmith's shop. As he glided over the floor, he felt his skin pricked by a file lying there. In a rage, he turned round upon it and tried to dart his fangs into it; but he could do no harm to heavy iron and had soon to give over his wrath.

It is useless attacking the insensible. (*Aesop, Sixth century B.C)*

There are some things in life you just can't change and, even if you could, you shouldn't. Our experiences mold us. It's how we become who we're meant to be.

I came from a very religious family, who sheltered me. In 1976, I met my husband in my freshman year of college. We shared several classes and became very good friends. He was the first man to ever pay attention to me and spend time with me. In spring of 1977, my family moved to Florida. I got my first kiss goodbye. I transferred to a Florida college. We kept in touch. When we were writing letters back and forth, I remember he wrote me that he was struggling with his roommates. He found out only after the fact that they were gay. I showed the letter to my friends, and we decided we weren't going to call him on it but ask leading questions to see how he'd respond. All the while, he held to his story that he just wasn't comfortable.

Though apart, we kept in touch. By the end of our college careers, we attended each other's graduations. That was 1980. He commented that there were no jobs in Mass. I offered that there were plenty of jobs in FL. So, without a word to his family, he packed every worldly possession and moved. He lived with my parents until he could get on his feet. I lived with my sister in a studio apartment on the beach.

Our relationship just "was." We never had the spark. We never had that rip-your-clothes-off-gotta-have-you experience, ever. We never really dated. We were just part of each other's lives. Every now and then, we went out on dates alone. Usually we were with a group.

I remember having a conversation with a family friend saying that if the relationship isn't going to go anywhere, I just need to let it go. I had my apt; he had his. I'd stay with him because I was in a studio with my sister. We initially weren't sexually active, not for a very long time. I remember going over to see him. He was in the shower, and I went in to join him. He asked me to leave. Back then, I figured it was me, and he let me believe that. I remember all the time feeling inadequate. He was all I knew. He was my one and only. The family friend must have had a conversation with him saying that, if he didn't do something, he would lose me. Years later, I found out that he was afraid he would lose me so he asked me to marry him.

You know if you have to coerce a relationship, you shouldn't get into it. By June 1981, we were engaged and married in June 1982. I remember my parents saying to me he was perfect for me. We had so much in common, a great friendship. In the early days, they would joke around and said, if I was ever so foolish to divorce him, they'd keep him and let me go.

For the most part, that's how life went. We followed socially expected time frames. We married, bought a house, had kids, etc. He did what he thought was expected. His father's approval meant a lot to him. He knew what was expected of him and thought that's how he would earn and keep his father's respect.

He was a rule follower. He loved structure and was very successful in these environments. He was very competitive, active in organized sports as well as chorus. For all outward appearances, he was Mr. All American.

Married life was quite stagnant. Within the first two years, I knew something wasn't quite right; but it took a long time to figure out that something was really missing and things became expected and routine. There was no natural affection, intimacy, or playfulness. Because my emotional needs weren't met, I ended up having to make rules early, early on. It became rote and lost its meaning. He had to tell me, "I love you," first thing in the morning and before we went to bed. We had no spontaneous affection. I always had to be the one to reach for his hand to hold it or to put my arm around him first to snuggle. He was sterile, stoic, unaffected.

We had our first child, miscarried a second pregnancy, carried the third pregnancy to term, and our second child was born. He was an amazing father. He loved being a daddy. He changed diapers, burped, and fed them. I think he really enjoyed that piece of family life. Married life? It was empty. He was a great dad, great provider, and yet I'm sitting here saying, there's something wrong. There were many key points where I'd tell him I wanted to go for counseling, and he'd make excuses, then become super dad, super husband. My friend called it "The Gerbil Wheel." Once we got back into our routine, all those "super" things fell away.

There was always a disconnect. I never felt like he was really part of us. When did I discover gay? I think it all began when his father moved away. His mother committed suicide, and, soon after, his father died of cancer. This life-altering event caused a huge shift and triggered a downward spiral. Still, I trusted him. His trips away became more frequent, and I would often call when he was away, and he would sometimes not pick up or not call and make excuses.

I was committed for the long haul. I used to tease... "The only way out of this marriage is in a pine box." Weird things would happen, but I wasn't ready to address them. I was in denial for many years. Both my sisters went through a divorce. It was ugly and painful, and I never wanted to experience it.

Ten years into our marriage, the Internet entered out lives. We got a $600 bill. The shame of it all was that he tried to blame it on our youngest daughter. He never did admit to it. Our eldest daughter knew and was afraid to tell me. I started getting more savvy, checked the history, and saw some gay sites, pictures of men. So I called him on it. He made excuses, and I remember telling him if he ever brought that into our home, we were over.

At that point, he was going to conferences in Tallahassee and Jacksonville. His gay life went underground, and he went deeply in the closet. I remember a credit card charge, calling the card company, and investigating it. They sent me a copy of the receipt with his signature, which was for an adult entertainment store. He never took responsibility for it.

2005-ish, our youngest was in HS, our oldest was in college, and we went to Sanibel Island for our anniversary. The first night was good. The second night, he couldn't make love, couldn't get an erection. I told him you are either going to counseling or we need to divorce. He tried to convince me that everything would be ok, that we'd work it out.

We didn't work it out. What did happen was his health changed. He started getting reactions to mosquito bites that he'd never done before. He was losing weight and looking pale. He went to an MD and told me about it after the fact. They wanted him to have an HIV test. I didn't understand why they wanted him to do that. He wouldn't talk about it. That was the beginning of the end. July 2006, he came home, waited for the house to be empty except for the two of us, and started crying. He told me the HIV test came back positive. He wanted me to hear it from him before the health dept. called. I have a high profile job, and this news could have been devastating.

It was a very, very dark time. I cannot describe the depth of despair, humiliation. I told no one, not my sisters, not my friends. I totally withdrew. I was sobbing when I went to see my gynecologist. She said, "You know, just because he is positive doesn't mean you are."

The wait for the results was hell. I remember crying like it was never going to stop, being so stressed at work and my friends not knowing. It was horrible. He could never tell me when he thought he contracted it and tried to play it off on a colonoscopy. I told him we'd sue the doctor, so he never pursued it.

I wanted to tell my sisters when I got my first clearance. Then the holidays arrived, then, let's wait again…then, telling myself, "You're living a lie. Everything you do is a lie."

February 2007, we were having problems with my youngest. We weren't yelling, just on egg shells, and it was very hard. I used that as an excuse to find a counselor for my daughter, and it ended up being for me. It was the best investment I ever made. I told her all about the dynamics. The girls still didn't know about their dad. My faith got me through the dark days, and the counselor pulled me out. She gave me permission to do – for me.

March, I had a conversation with my husband to separate. We talked to the girls during their spring break. The youngest was in shock, and, to the oldest, it was no surprise. I finally got the courage to ask him if he would ever be able to love me the way I needed to be loved. He didn't respond. I found an attorney who just happened to also be a str8 spouse. I put down a binder and filed after 25 years of marriage. I served him divorce papers on our 25th wedding anniversary. I had to deal with the reality that my husband may not have ever loved me and that twenty-some odd years of my life were a lie. It took me to my knees.

It was shortly thereafter that our oldest was home from college, and her dad was working out in the yard. She found medicine in the fridge and looked it up online. She called me, hysterical, asking, "Why is Dad taking medicine for HIV?"

I called him and told him he needed to tell her the truth. He went into the house and said, "What do you want to know?"

She wanted honesty, and he told her he had HIV, and he didn't know how he got it, and that he was never unfaithful to her mother.

What we've learned is that persons who cannot be honest with themselves cannot be honest with anyone else. We stopped expecting it. He is not capable of facing his reality nor taking accountability for it.

Insight? What can I offer? You are not alone. You're not the only one. Truly, it's not about you. Don't own their dysfunction. Don't let it define you. You determine, you decide who you are, who you want to be and live that way, regardless of what they say, do, or what happens.

Healing for everyone is a journey, especially when children are dealing with this issue. Children are still children, regardless of their age. The oldest child is working on acceptance. She still misses the "daddy" she thought she had and knew and wants him to be honest. She's angry. The youngest accepts that situation but won't accept gay until he concretely comes out. They both love him and miss him but seriously question what was true and what was a lie. They often question if their daddy still loves them and if he ever did. The sad thing is that both children are ok with it, so we can't figure out what's holding him back from being honest. He's wasting precious time. I encourage the girls to see their father as often as possible as there's no telling how long he will be here. I'm saddened by the words I threw out into the universe..."The only way out of this marriage is in a pine box."

Rudy…

As I sit here reflective, preparing to write about those dark days at the beginning of this journey and times since, one thing is overwhelmingly evident. I AM here, just as another straight spouse promised at my first Straight Spouse Network gathering. Miles and years of steady baby steps later, I have reinvented and defined my self, my life, my perspective, and, most of all, my peace of mind.

During early 1999, my work involved traveling all over to prepare computers for the impending doom of Y2K. Little did I know that while I traveled, my wife (then 39) stayed home with the boys, (ages 15 and 17), and discovered herself with her seventy-year-old girl friend. I was 41. We'd been married nineteen years. My new job involved working at home, and I thought this would be my great chance to right things and get closer to my wife. What I found out was how deeply involved she was with her girlfriend. On October 28, she told me she was gay. My immediate reaction was relief. At last, everything that happened over the previous ten months instantly made sense, like a solution to a math equation suddenly becoming clear and sensible.

For three days, I walked around days relieved. Then I had to face what she was asking of me. She wanted to be gay and have me as the front man guarding the closet door. Everything would be normal, except she'd leave every night and return before the kids got up. This horrible secret festered. My counselor and I started working on the root of the problem: I couldn't stand guard at this post. It wasn't in me, no matter how much I wanted my marriage to go on. Once I reached a point where I couldn't stand it, I forced the issue. She came out to the kids and then moved out of the house.

There's a three-month blur of this most difficult time ever in my life. I can't remember ever crying so much. I showered a lot so the kids wouldn't know. I couldn't sleep and took medicine that made me shake so badly I could hardly put food in my mouth. Later, I changed to a milder anti-depressant and started riding my bike daily. My salvation was face-to-face contacts with other straight spouses and the Str8s online list.

I found a girlfriend, who introduced me to Buddhism. Something clicked and made sense. I opened my mind to something special I'd gone my whole life searching. The lessons were exactly what I needed and right on time. Although the girlfriend didn't last, I'm still a Buddhist.

The next year, I attended my first Florida gathering of straight spouses, my first exposure to a large group of them and all that a gathering is about: cooking and drinking and even laughter. The fellowship was something I hadn't experienced since the Army. Afterwards, I started corresponding with Sandy, whom I met there. We went to another gathering and had an excellent time. Later, we decided we liked each other and began a relationship. In 2001, she moved next door, and I started divorce proceedings.

A few months later, I was laid off and launched my real estate career. This was a huge decision, one that my old life and ex-wife would never have allowed. It's something for which I've found I have a gift and the most enjoyable job since training soldiers.

Last year, Sandy and I pulled off our surprise wedding at the by now annual Florida gathering. It was magical, for me, a sign that I really do have a new life and I'm sharing it with a wonderful woman, something I'd not thought possible. My life today is because my former wife is a lesbian and Sandy's ex-husband is gay. (2006, retrieved from www.straightspouse.org).

Helen Platero…

I met Sean my first semester in college. He was several years older than me, but just starting out as well. Our friendship slowly developed into a relationship, and we moved in together. We were married right after graduation. The next few years were difficult, which I attributed to stress and to being starving graduate students. We seemed close, and all our friends described us as the perfect couple. Yet in hindsight, I can see that we were leading two separate lives.

During my last year of graduate school, Sean became obsessed with buying a house. I had absolutely no time to devote to this, but it became his mission. We moved into our dream house six months before my graduation. I was so busy with school that I didn't even help with the moving process.

I landed my dream job right after graduation. Sean was already established in his profession, and we were finally on the right track. For the first time in years, I felt like I could breathe. One month later, it all came crashing down when he disclosed to me that he was gay.

I was completely blindsided. I had absolutely no idea. We had plenty of gay friends, and he seemed comfortable in his sexuality. Instead, he had been completely closeted and desperate for absolutely no one to know. His plan was never to disclose, but to commit suicide instead. He finally told a sibling who convinced him to confess to me.

In retrospect, I could see the signs. We never had the intimacy that I craved. I blamed that on myself and my conservative upbringing. I internalized all of the baggage and grew to think that I was flawed and unattractive. Our marriage would be better if I were a better wife or a better cook or if I were less needy or if I were less emotional

Once he disclosed, he went running back into the closet, and I was dragged right into it with him. I wasn't allowed to tell anyone what was going on and was supposed to act like everything was fine. This lasted for two long years until I became depressed and withdrawn. I can't bear to look at a single photo of my self from that period – I was the walking dead.

Sean's behavior was becoming more erratic. He went on spending binges and began to drink heavily. He went through a series of jobs and finally became unemployed and left me. Weeks later, we had an argument that ended with him trying to take his life. I had him hospitalized and spent all of my energy helping him, instead of grieving the end of my marriage.

It was during this period that I found the Straight Spouse Network. I spent years believing I was the only person that this had ever happened to and instead found many others in my situation. My feelings and fears were validated. I could start the process of healing. I had to re-learn years of faulty thinking and emotional abuse.

We were divorced one year later, and I remained close to him and his family. He was diagnosed as bipolar and that created a whole new set of issues. I found love again, and, while it wasn't meant to be, it helped me on the road to healing.

Five years after our separation, Sean came to me and asked me to be his "best woman" at the commitment ceremony he was having with his partner. I declined and offered to give him away instead. It was a cleansing experience for me as I symbolically and emotionally gave him away. I could then begin my period of detachment in earnest.

One year later, I physically detached myself from the relationship by moving cross-country. Now, I could focus on me and what I wanted from this life. I let go of the guilt I felt from my part in this suicide attempt. I shared my experiences with other straight spouses and helped their roads to recovery.

I will always love the man I married, but can no longer help him. I expend that energy now on me and my happiness. Through this long journey, I realize that I love the person I've become.

Mike...

She packed the van and drove off. The kids were already asleep in their beds, and I returned to my glass of wine. Modesto, of all places -- she was on the way to Modesto to pursue a woman with whom she'd had a six-month affair a year before we met and fell in love – eighteen years ago. Fourteen years ago, we were married. Now, after reconnection with this woman, she was on her way to see her. There was no doubt as to why she was going. They'd been texting, e-mailing, and speaking on the phone for the last three months. In fact, she was very truthful, stating she needed to go, needed to see this woman. I told her I would not sit across from her when she was 75 years old and have her hate me because I held her back from something. I knew in the deepest recesses of my mind and the bottom of my heart that it was over. She had proposed that maybe she could see her twice a year or be free to explore her sexuality within the marriage. I considered these possibilities would uphold my vows and my convictions that a family should be intact. These options were not on the table for long.

She returned and said literally nothing. She slept on the couch for the next three months and then filed for divorce. I asked about marriage counseling; she stated she was already seeing a counselor. I asked if we could find someone to see us together. She said, "No," but invited me to see her counselor with her.

I looked the counselor up online: she was aligned with the San Jose Gay and Lesbian Center. On a Wednesday morning, I sat with my soon-to-be-ex-wife and her therapist for 45 minutes. The therapist stated plainly that my marriage was over, that Kathie no longer loved me, and that reconciliation was not an option. Kathie sat across from me, silent and sobbing. I left, devastated, disoriented, and consumed with sadness, fear, and anger.

Kathie told our close friends and family that she had the affair and we were getting divorced. My parents were crushed. They had adored her and our supposed idyllic family life. Friends were split. So much sympathy came towards Kathie for the years she'd spent hiding her true feelings that my anger grew. I got into counseling, started on anti-anxiety and depression medication, and even went to AA. Half way through my Twelve Step process, my sponsor asked if I would like to talk a bit more about my alcohol use instead of my divorce.

I sought out friends, learned who my true friends were, strengthened bonds with family, and found the Straight Spouse Network. I reflected on how I had lost myself so many years ago, how Kathie's homosexuality had permeated our marriage and my life and had made me miserable, unhappy, and unpleasant to be around.

Mediation was quick. Despite our difficulty with intimate relations, our partnership had been a success. I asked that she never set foot in the family home again. She asked for my 401k; I asked that she pay off all credit card debts. There was never a question that we wouldn't share equal custody of our children. So, with surgical precision, we reached a divorce settlement. Our mediator congratulated us on how we handled the process. What could be done? What could be said? My partner of eighteen years wanted to have sex with women; why prolong anything?

We told the kids and gave them the answer they and we could handle: "Sometimes people don't get along. It has nothing to do with you. Mommy and Daddy will always love you the same. You did nothing wrong; we just don't love each other anymore." With the stability we gave them and support from extended family, they seem to be doing well. She moved into a rental down the street, so they can ride their scooters back and forth. Even the dog goes back and forth now.

Disorientation, disbelief were the first feelings. I stumbled through my days, waking every once in a while to wonder if it was a dream. I replayed this for months. We had a family, we'd been married for fourteen years, and we'd been great partners. Had this really happened? I asked everyone I trusted, sometimes several times during the day, "Did this really happen? Is she really leaving? Does she really want to start over at 40? Does she really want to love women?" I struggled with these feelings for months. Denial, is that what this is called?

Anger was there, too. How could she do this? Had I not given the best I could, for years? How could she do this? I gave her all of the space within this marriage that I could have. In hindsight, I gave her an incredible amount of space, so much that my anger turned on me for not reading the signs and standing up before I did, after the three months that she spent on the couch. Why didn't I stand up? Where was I while all of this was going on? Why did I stand for this for so long, try to reconcile until the end, when she had made up her mind months, maybe even years ago?

Jealousy, also. There she was, moving into a new role, welcomed by the support of her family, some of our friends and a community ready to welcome her into her new role. She was seen as being tortured during this relationship, living incorrectly. Now there were many people ready to support her and her new life. She even lashed out at me, calling me angry, antisocial, and mean. While I was left to pick up the pieces, who was there to welcome me into ...... heterosexuality? It seems that the culture is very open and accepting, which is wonderful. I have no prejudices, live and let live. But real harm was done, real harm fueled by lies, perpetuated over years, by Kathie. It does not seem right for someone to lie to themselves and those closest to them for years and then gain absolution so quickly.

Confusion and being emasculated were other major emotions. What does this mean for me as a man? I was confident before. I was successful. I worked hard away from home, and I worked hard at home. Our sex life had always been strained: I have a high sex drive; she never did, for very obvious reasons. We tried to be respectful and meet in the middle. I felt like I took care of her. I pleased her, and she pleased me. Everything now had been brought into question. She was repulsed and had been for years. I now questioned everything about our sex life. What could I have done differently? Had she ever been attracted to me? How was I going to move forward, knowing this was the outcome?

As I move through this slowly, these issues are resolving. It is real: she did choose to become or realize she was gay in the middle of her life. I see the evidence. She lives around the corner, so it's inevitable. My anger has subsided, kept in check by the fact that I have a new life and I am the one that controls my thoughts and feelings. If anger were what I feel, that is what I will project, and I will be alone.

I am no longer jealous. I'm also no longer confused. She is a separate person. I thought I exerted some control over her or knew how she was feeling or what she was thinking. You cannot truly know what any person is thinking or feeling. These things must be talked about, shared and nurtured together.

I have taken control of my life. I've changed my role and now enjoy connections that I have not before. I strengthened bonds between family and friends and now have a network instead of relying on a partner. I met a patient and loving woman to whom I gave honesty about where I was, and she gave me understanding. She has become part of my life, of my healing. I am now confident in my role as a man. And that role has grown so much. I consider myself a better father, brother, son, and partner.

Tessa...

But behavior in the human being is sometimes a defense, a way of concealing motives and thoughts, as language can be a way of hiding your thoughts and preventing communication. (Maslow, retrieved from http://thinkexist.com)

I'm from the islands. We are raised to be respectful, giving, faithful to God, and loyal to our family. I discovered early in my marriage that these were things my husband desired but could not do for me nor for himself. I'm not quite divorced, 30 years old. I'm now in school to be a physician's assistant. I was married to my husband only five years. We met through a mutual friend, dated, and, in 2005, were married. He joined the military. I saw it as a stable career with great benefits. I supported his new career move and put my own educational needs on hold.

I had no idea my husband was gay. Everyone loved him. He was the quiet type and often kept to himself. He said he never had a lot of girlfriends. I thought he was just shy. I remember his friend who introduced us later told me that his brother had asked her, "Find him a woman before he turns gay."

Evidently, truer things are said in jest. I found out later that most people thought he was gay. No one had the courage to tell me.

I didn't get disclosure right away; I got depression, anger, violence, lies, and an emotional vacuum at first. How did it all begin? We were just newlyweds, and I found gay porn on our computer. He made excuses, telling me he was just comparing sizes.

How was married life? I saw a much different side to him early on. It seemed he could laugh and experience joy with everyone but me. Married life was lonely and filled with angst. He never wanted to go anywhere nor do anything with me. I could see he was happy and, the moment he walked in the door, he was depressed and angry. He just wanted to come home after work, eat, and watch TV. There wasn't any excitement. We didn't have a social life. I couldn't figure out why he couldn't experience any joy with me. The strangest part was that we had an active sex life. Looking back on it, I often wonder if he was trying to get his "fix" sexually with me, hoping that would somehow satisfy his needs and desires. I think he was testing the waters to see if he could make a straight marriage work.

I also think finding the gay porn was the tip of the iceberg. Looking back on it, I think he was looking for a soul mate. He was searching desperately for that relationship he needed, which he just couldn't get with me, well, honestly, any woman. I think he would have married any woman that would have agreed to say, "I do." He needed, wanted, and desired to be with a man and kept a lot of distraction in our lives to keep my eyes off that desire.

By 2008, we'd moved three times. We finally seemed to find a place to call home, so I enrolled in school to finish my undergraduate work in biology. I started to see a real change in him, and the pain of being married to him was unbearable. I made Dean's List that semester because I never wanted to go home. I went to class and stayed in the library till it closed every night to avoid having to deal with the isolation and loneliness.

The one who never wanted to leave his home started going out by himself and staying out late during the week. He planned weekends for himself away. One weekend, he drove from VA to Philadelphia to drop his guy off. He wouldn't even go to my sister's wedding with me. One time during this separate lifestyle, I took ill with the flu. I had to practically beg him to go buy me some vapor rub. He was upset since that meant he had to swing back home instead of going directly to pick up his guy. Had I not been so weak, I would never have asked him.

I am a woman of faith and could not bear this on my own. I returned to church. My priest was my spiritual guide and counselor. He helped me find my way back to God. My faith saved me. It was only when I focused on the things of God and not of the world that I could see the world objectively. I could see that I didn't cause my husband's hurt, pain, and anger. I could look upon him and not feel the loss, rejection, and loneliness that I had been so stricken with for so long. I could finally accept that my husband didn't want me, not because of me, but because he was gay, and I endured abuses because he could not cope with himself. A weight lifted off my shoulders when I really understood that his misery was not about me.

He was always complaining that he hated the military, hated life, hated me -- all in the name of hiding the person he wanted to be. I realize now he was taking it all out on me and somehow was blaming me for the fact that he was in his own self-imposed closet.

I also found out early on that he was filled with deep-rooted anger, the kind of anger that is built up over years of stuffing regret, struggle, and angst. It was an anger completely disconnected from me and our marriage. I was the whipping post and nothing more. It was the anger that led him to place locks on all of his belongings, to place passwords on his phone and computer. It was this anger that fueled him to hit me and threaten me. It was this anger that taught me that he had issues that were far beyond me and my ability to help him as his wife.

We had a family wedding to attend Christmas, 2009. He refused to go, making the excuse he didn't want to use all his vacation time. While I was there, he called to tell me he had something to tell me. I was thinking for sure he'd found someone else. I had my suspicions, at first, thinking it was another woman and stewing on that before my arrival home.

Once home, I had the blinders off. I prayed a lot, asking God for guidance, for strength, for the ability to do His will, knowing that this marriage would never allow me to become the person I needed to be to truly serve Him. I prayed for the insight to see past my husband's lies and to accept the truth that he was not the man he said he was at the altar.

He chose the precious minutes before midnight New Year's Eve 2009 to tell me he'd found someone else. We were home watching the ball drop in Times Square. I surprised myself when I said matter of fact, "Oh, a guy, right?" At that moment, it was midnight. His phone rang. His friend actually called to wish him Happy New Year, and my husband had the audacity to pick up the phone and take the call. He left me on the couch to go talk to his friend. I was sobbing.

The next day and the day after that and the day after that, he was gone. He was out all the time and never made time for "us" ever again. It hurt so much to see him come home and get excited about going out, when he never did that with me. He abandoned me. He went as far as to disconnect my line from our "family plan" and add his guy. I was sitting there, wondering how come no one called me to wish me happy holidays, and decided to call my mom, only to get the disconnection notice! Mind you, this was my line that I'd changed to a family plan and added him.

The more I attended church, the more I was able to see everything objectively. I could understand all his dysfunctional behavior was due to his need to live his gay lifestyle. He treated me horrible because he could; I was the safe one. I'm not sure why guilt was a heavy burden on my heart. I felt guilty that I was angry, and I hated the fact he was so happy and I was so alone. I spent a lot of time with my priest to work through those feelings, realizing eventually that it was because I knew we needed to divorce. He needed to find himself. I knew he would always use me to hide, and marriage was not the place. Marriage is supposed to be a place where you support each other, love each other, and enjoy each other. It's a place you build memories and a life. I often thank God that we didn't have any children.

One day, I asked him to tell me about his friend, and you would have thought he was a child on Christmas morning. He told me all about his friend. He opened up to me and, for the first time, I saw joy in his eyes. It was the kind of joy that comes from deep within. It was genuine. It was that defining moment that I knew we needed to end our marriage.

He had other ideas. He wanted us to stay married, live in separate rooms, and live separate lives. I couldn't do it. I stayed only because I didn't have anywhere to go. I knew I had to finish my Bachelor's then apply for med school. I knew enough to do something for me and my future and then make decisions about my marriage. He isolated me. I graduated in December 2009.

How did the marriage come to an end? It was summer 2009, just about the time he had orders to go to Iraq. I was looking for tools for a household project and knew they were in his truck, which was always open and not locked. I was ironically looking for a hammer and found documents instead. I was horrified. Evidently, his sister had instructed him to get his things in order and to change all of his personal documents to make sure that I didn't get anything should anything happen to him. I found his life insurance policy, retirement information, and will, in which nothing was left to me. He'd changed all the beneficiary information. I was numb. I reached in the truck further and found that he had copies of my personal journal. The journal was spiritual and also a record of everything I'd endured. Finding this revealed the reality of the depth of his misery. He knew he couldn't be trusted so therefore I couldn't either; and he evidently spent countless hours sifting through my belongings, looking for any reason to hold something against me to justify his own path and wave of destruction.

When I showed him the papers I'd found, he was violent with me. He threw me to the floor, yelling, "I'm going to kill you."

I was looking up at him and not reacting.

He was insane. He was banging my head on the floor. "Are you happy now?" he kept yelling over and over.

I remember standing up when I could and looking at the spot where I had been on the floor. I had been right next to a work out machine. I remember thanking God my husband hadn't smashed my head on it. When I got up and away from him, I called the police and his commanding officer. I had him arrested.

When he came back, he took the keys to my car. I called his commander. His commander got him on the phone. The moment he was on the phone with his commander, it was "No sir," "Yes, sir." It was "Jekyll and Hyde." I think he needed the structure and discipline of the military because he didn't have it for himself. He had no self-control, so he wanted to control me.

As soon as he got off the phone with his commander, he screamed and yelled and threatened me again. I reached for the phone. He stopped yelling and threw the car keys at me. It was a tantrum, and I was Mommy. Interestingly enough, when he was calm, he often blamed his anger issues on being raised in such a strict house. I think "strict" had a whole new meaning. I think he knew he was gay, he told his family, and they couldn't accept it, which forced him to live a "straight" life and live a life where he couldn't be true to himself.

Once he came out, I ended up telling my mom the truth. They were planning a visit and I didn't want to have to figure out reasons why he was never home and never wanted to spend time with the family. By this time, he had his own life established and wanted nothing to do with me.

I vacillate with wanting to ask him questions. People I run into have stories for me about my soon-to-be-ex-husband. An old neighbor told me my husband had men in our home. Part of me wants to know; then, part of me doesn't. I don't need to know "what" in order to have closure. I don't know if I want to put myself through all that pain.

A friend of his family told me that they are saying that the reason we broke up was because I found out he was buying gifts for another woman. Another story is that I only married him to get my green card. It was so far from the truth, but he said anything to discredit me.

I already feel a sense of closure because I know our marriage won't work and we are divorcing. I know why he's so angry, and I understand his issues. It wasn't so easy under the roof though. He often manipulated me with the Bible, knowing I'm a Christian. When I asked for the separation, he told me I was judging him and that a true Christian wouldn't judge another.

The pretzel logic astounds me. Had I been able to think clearly, I would have said, "But you have sex with men. You don't want me. God wants more for me and has rules for how husbands should treat their wives."

However, at that time...I was in a different place...I wasn't thinking about me...I was only thinking about him...and somehow he made me feel guilty. I'd thought, "Well, since he's not attracted to me, maybe it could work as an open marriage."

That didn't last long. During the week, I'd had school. Weekends, I had to stay home and sit home, watching him go out and be happy. So I'd started to go to church more and got the courage to talk to the priest. The more I went for spiritual counsel, I realized it was all manipulation and it would never work. He'd compromised my entire belief system. My faith changed. It got stronger. It became so much easier... I found it easier to accept, forgive.

We were talking about the separation agreement ... he punched the wall. There was a hole in it... he had to fill it.... Once he calmed down, we worked out the terms. The agreement was that when he got back from Iraq, I had to leave, July 2010. He had the house from then on.

I moved, June 2010... He had the nerve to call me to come pick him up from the airport. No one was there to get him. I did. He did not reenlist in the military. He was discharged in August.

I think a lot about the grieving process and am really at the acceptance stage of it all. I think, while I was married, I was processing through the denial, bargaining, anger. It takes time to work through everything you endure. I remember bargaining early on. I asked God if He can take away the gay, take it out of my husband's head (that's how he mentioned it -- as "in his head" and he couldn't get it out), then we would return to Him and live a faithful life to Him. I told Him I knew I could then be a better wife.

I'd bargained with my husband's military career, saying to myself, "If I invest myself in him now, we'll have a solid future. I can deal with his anger if I know I'll be taken care of financially."

When the relationship turned for the worst, I made strides to return to school. I'd always put it off and knew I couldn't any longer. I had bargained, "If I just put him first now, I'll get my education later, and we'll both have great careers: him in the military and me with a degree in medicine." That's not where I am anymore. I have a year till I graduate from med school. My future is just that, mine.

Morris...

I was 27 when I met my wife, twenty-two years ago. I'd been through several important relationships and felt I knew myself very well at that point. When I met her, I realized she was exactly the kind of person I would like to spend my life with – independent, intelligent, open-minded. The only thing missing was a strong sexual attraction. I told myself that was not important or perhaps would come with time and love. I had been raised by a very strong mother who looked down on sexual desire, and I thought I experienced strong sexual desire with girlfriends. I held a strong belief that a "good" man did not care about such things. Within a month of starting to date, she told me two very significant and personal things: she was bisexual and that her one true love affair had been with a woman (the men she dated she wasn't sexual with and didn't feel attracted to), and she believed she had been sexually abused.

I was supportive of her in both regards. In retrospect, I ascribed our lack of sexual chemistry to her possible abuse history rather than her ambivalence toward the male body. As to bisexuality, we both felt it simply meant that she could be happy with someone of either gender. She shortly began therapy for abuse and, in the long run, came to the conclusion that she had not been abused but had suffered through a cold and emotionally empty childhood.

We married nineteen-plus years ago even though her attraction to women – friends, co-workers, my co-workers – was already apparent. I tried to remain open-minded, but it was not until she asked to visit her old lover and strike up their relationship anew that I realized how powerful these feelings were. I did not react well. I've always been monogamous and expected the same. She dropped the subject but was sill quietly attracted to new women over and over.

Again, in retrospect, I should have noticed the patterns that were developing – her lack of interest in sex with me and my pretending I didn't care – which led us to a stressful sexual relationship. Although I could masturbate daily, I almost never initiated sex. We would be sexual once or twice a month at most. The act of sex became not so much part of our spectrum of connection and affection as an isolated event we had to do to be truly married.

Fast forward through a dozen years of child-rearing, career-building, etc., during which "the gay thing" seemed to subside and vanish. Through the hard work and life-building, we were closer in many ways, and our physical affection and sexual relationship had settled into an uneasy, but acceptable, equilibrium.

Around our fifteenth anniversary, my wife suddenly began to feel much more sexual, and our relationship blossomed. I felt like all the years of patience and waiting paid off. A better sexual relationship translated into many other feelings: a deeper trust in the marriage, more non-sexual affection, and more emotional connection. For her, it was also bringing up gay feelings. Almost three years ago, she told me of her ache, the empty place I could not fill, and implied that she'd like to seek a lover. I reacted even worse than before. I was devastated, certain we would fail. I began reading about mixed-orientation marriages, which led me to a stronger *place.*

While I knew intellectually it was not about me, there were still esteem issues, things I thought that I might have done differently. Really, though, these thoughts about what I should have done had been present all along. Now they were conscious.

The major issues were and still are: How do I reconcile my desire for monogamy and her desire for non-monogamy? (How do I lovingly let her be who she needs to be when that is not what I want in a marriage?) How do I learn to express and honor who "I" am sexually, while trying to be who she can accept me being sexually? How do I reconcile my intense desire to live with my children when the answer to all the questions above continues to be – "I can't "?

It was almost immediately clear that, if she stuffs her feelings and desires, our relationship suffers. Yet, if she were to act upon her feelings, I wouldn't want to be part of the marriage. Where was room for compromise? In talking to a number of other people in similar circumstances, I learned a lot about myself -- like being knocked out of a comfortable rut and forced to take a real look at the landscape of my life. I realized I am a good man, father, and husband. I realized that I place the greatest value on being there for my four children and that I'm not willing to live apart from them.

With the help of the straight wife of a gay husband, I realized that what I am is natural and that my sexual desire is normal and healthy: I am a sexual person and not willing to pretend I'm not. (To be clear, ours was a non-sexual friendship.) I want to be desired physically, as well as emotionally. My wife says she is 70-percent attracted to women compared to men, though I would wager the percentage is higher. Finally, I find a great deal of my emotional bonding comes through sexual intimacy.

It took almost two years, but I eventually pushed for marriage counseling. I went into counseling feeling like we needed to find a way to separate, as I could see no other path forward. I was tired of the unsolvable holding pattern. Sex was more stressful than ever – we seemed to feel we had to prove to ourselves that we could do it and that we had to, in order to stay married. It took a lot for me to overcome that feeling of not being wanted, knowing that she fantasized about women, and to just focus on the emotional closeness and physical sensation of it. Neither of us was very present.

The initial focus of counseling was not on solving "the problem," but on looking at what works and doesn't in our relationship. We are very emotionally supportive, caring and respectful, and excellent partners together. As we started working on non-sexual intimacy, my wife expressed affection, but even going out and having fun with me is often clouded by her fear that I might be thinking about wanting to be sexual later. It felt threatening to her. So we stated that we would stop having sex for a while.

Placing the moratorium on sexual activity was a revelation. The amount of stress it relieved was incredible. That fact that I still cared for her and was willing to stay in the house with her was more than important – it was vital. I came to realize that I was willing to let her have what she needs and try an open marriage. Some things I tried to be clear about, like the fact that I can't see rebuilding a sex life with her under the same stressful conditions we had over the past two decades. Also, I'm not interested in a casual sexual relationship. If I was to become emotionally and sexually involved with someone else, I would be pulled farther away from my wife. Yet I also want to live in the house with her and the children (our youngest is just 7). We could slowly drift apart into being close, caring co-parents. We haven't had sex in months and that feels right. My wife thinks things will go differently and sees no barrier to us resuming sex even if other people are part of our intimate lives. I disagree.

We are officially an open marriage, though neither of us has acted on it. We're early in this opening up process, and she has a lot of work to do to open her mind to embrace her sexuality after all these years. She has a great deal of fear over family, friends, work, and the reactions that would follow if she were to fully come out. I know that some of her motivation for wanting to remain married is to keep some of that at bay, and a part of me wants to protect her. So it will be some time before anything happens, though I don't want to place a time table on anything and don't see that going slow or fast will make any difference to me.

I am at peace, quite surprising, given how I felt two years ago. There is a large element of "Let's get on with it. Let's see what happens." The holding pattern was terrible. To be honest, I'm not confident we will go into old age together, but I also know that if we split, I'll survive on my own. If it turns out one or both of us would be better off with other people, then it will be *good to know.*

I want to emphasize how important my wife's honesty and patience has been. She has not cheated, and she encouraged me to go through my own process. I'd offered to give her an open marriage a few years ago, but she knew I didn't mean it. I can't say enough about her understanding. I really want her to be happy. I also want me to be happy. Time will tell.

Delilah...

We went to college together, students at the same university. I was a Communications major, and he was an Accounting and Business major. A mutual friend introduced us. We were friends for a couple years and in a committed relationship in our senior year, 1995. We lived off campus. After graduation, we started living together and were engaged in 1996. While we were dating, he tried to break it off. This was shortly after a fight where we didn't speak for a few days and I stayed with a friend. Then we got engaged. We were married in 1998 in a lavish ceremony with 400 guests. When we were living together, even before the marriage, there was tension and a lot of fighting over the littlest things. He'd be angry for a couple days at a time. He was unsettled, unhappy. Initially, I thought it was me. I didn't think he was gay; I just thought something was different. He threatened divorce every time we got into a fight. He knew.

Our marriage was apparently "normal." We entertained. We had friends. Once we bought our home, our Halloween parties were legendary.

I suspected in 2005. I now jokingly call it the "7 year switch." After a big fight, it seemed he was much too angry for the subjects we were discussing. He said, "I'm not attracted to you. My life with you is a lie. I'm only with you because you wanted to work it out."

Then something in me clicked... no straight guy would say something like this.

He made a new friend. He said he met him at work. They did everything together. When I met this friend, the story my husband told me about him changed. He said they'd met at a big electronics retailer. The friend, who I'll call Deke, was giving my husband a lot of expensive gifts and gave me a board game for Christmas. I started going through Deke's stuff. I went through my husband's computer and found out Deke was a sex offender from California. I didn't say anything because then my husband would have known I was snooping. So I held to the saying, "Keep your friends close, your enemies closer," and accepted Deke's company and allowed him into our home. I needed to get to know him.

I needed that time to gather as much information as possible. I also planned a party for my husband. All this time, Deke was at the house. When my husband and Deke went shopping, I snooped through his suitcase. I found Viagra and ticket stubs from Brokeback Mountain. I'd really wanted to see that movie, and, when I'd previously asked my husband to go, he'd refused to see it with me, saying, "Why would anyone want to see a movie about two gay guys?"

I found a paycheck stub of Deke's. My husband had told me Deke was a contractor at the big company he works at. Deke wasn't. It turned out Deke was a manager at a chain restaurant. In his wallet was also a business card for a place called "SW" with my husband's contact info and work email address, written in his handwriting on the back. Later, I found a blue membership card with a logo with waves on it and the text, "SW." I asked a few str8 friends of mine to check it out, and they refused, after looking at the address. So called a gay friend of mine, who came out around the same time my husband and I had started dating. He confirmed it was a gay gym and bathhouse club where you had to be a member. At this point, I was making color copies of everything I found in his wallet. My friend went to the bathhouse, brought back a card, and it matched.

So my husband's relationship with Deke evolved, and my husband wanted Deke to spend a lot of time with us. I'm not sure if inviting me to be part of that was somehow due to his guilt. This part of it all I just couldn't understand.

2006 was a big year. In February, I found the SW card, called my friend to confirm that, yes, it really was a membership card for a gay bathhouse. Soon after, I did a Google search, where I found the Straight Spouse Network.

For close to 9 months, I was going through a lot of denial. I finally told my husband, "If there's another guy or gal, I'll let you go."

His first reaction was one of anger for me to even suggest a guy. He was unnaturally homophobic. He asked me about swinging. I thought it was a joke. It wasn't. So I spent the better part of the year gathering information and following him. He said he was going to a birthday party, and I saw him outside of the gay bathhouse with another guy. I realized this place was his regular haunt.

Through the support of the new friends I'd met, I finally got the courage to confront my husband. I called him and told him everything I knew and had found. He was very defensive. He finally admitted to everything. The next day, when I was back at the house, he was mortified I'd talked to his family because he was worried about what they'd think of him. He was never concerned about me.

I got tested, and, luckily, it was negative. I'll never forget having to do this.

There was this trip we had planned to Egypt. Deke was supposed to go. He backed out. He knew I knew everything. He got on the phone and apologized…and then told me how in love with my husband he really was. I went to Egypt with my husband, May 2006. I saw it as a closure trip. He wanted to have sex and patch up our marriage. I gave in and had sex. It was unprotected. I look back on that and just cringe. I had just been tested. I saw the trip as surreal. It was like an out-of-body experience. I compartmentalized everything to take in the fact I was going to see the pyramids, I was on the Nile, enjoying the food, the people, the culture, etc. I put aside the dynamics of what we didn't have anymore to take in the experience of the trip. The Egypt trip was the last hurrah.

He always wanted a really clean house. The first two years after this, we had a bunch of trees and we'd bag leaves. We spent all of our time, cleaning and preparing for parties. We separated emotionally. We were too busy cleaning to talk. We still shared the same bedroom for years. We were roommates, sleeping fully clothed on opposite sides of the bed. We started taking roommates in.

Eventually, he and Deke broke up, and he started dating a guy named Kevin. It was at this time that I started opening up to more people, telling my parents, friends etc.

We're still in the same house. He lives on one side; I live on the other. I'm in a new relationship, and eventually my significant other will move in with us until we save the money we want for the home we want. It's all temporary. My now ex-husband is fine with all of us living together. It isn't traditional, but what in life really is?

Do I have any parting words? No secrets. Everything's out in the open.

Chapter 5
"Soul" Survivor

The vignettes that follow reveal the inner conflicts and human dilemmas that arise for all of us. However, only these individuals in their particular circumstances can resolve these conflicts as they forge their ways through the fires where they find themselves. Some are in limbo, others in shock, still others paralyzed as they face moral or emotional dilemmas and try to discern, assess, and sort out the particular variables in their lives. Our hope is that these windows let you see and hear the issues that are uniquely theirs and how they felt about and coped with them. Each vignette presents a variation of personal crises most of us face at one time or another. Our goal is simply to share these women's and men's feelings, not to shock, call for judgment, or seek pity, but rather to tap your empathy, as a fellow traveler.

Think of it this way. Are you a cactus in the desert? You arm yourself with waxy, thick skin. Your knobby, knotted thorns protect you from emotional predators. Your razor sharp needles store the vital necessities of life, and your roots, oh your very deep roots, secure you through the unforeseen. The desert is like that; it's filled with the unforeseen. One cannot live for any great length of time in such unbearable and deplorable conditions. Whatever does exist in that parched land is viciously competitive for the very resources upon which you also rely.

It's a cyclical pain, day and night, living through extremes; yet some of us stay and endure like the cactus. Some cactus species can live up to 150 years adapting to their environment, somehow accepting their conditions. But, why do they? Why would you? Will you survive that long? How will you protect yourself being so vulnerable to the elements? How will you sustain your life?

Do you see that you're alive but that which surrounds you is barren and dry? So, instead of asking if you are you a cactus in the desert, quite possibly a better question is this: are we addicted to pain? Perhaps that's the question that only a cactus can answer.

Let's listen...

Joe...

"I was married 23 years and was never allowed to just snuggle and hold my wife in bed. She said I suffocated her. It was only until I met and fell in love with a straight woman that I was able to snuggle and hold someone till the sun came up."

Henry...

"My wife has never been passionate about us. We've been comfortable, like a favorite pair of shoes. We've never had got-to-have-you-rip-your-clothes-off sex ever. She won't have anything to do with foreplay. Sex is mechanical at best. I'm lonely. I never feel really wanted. It would be nice to feel passion."

Susie...

"I'm always the one to initiate sex."

Robin...

"She's never wanted or needed intimacy, not from me. It kills me. Everything I ever wanted from her, she gives to another woman."

Anonymous...

"When am I going to stop feeling sorry for myself? I can't believe this is happening. I can't stop wondering what my husband is doing when he's alone. Why did I do this to myself? Why can't I just let him go? Why can't I just tell him to leave? I can't tell you what the Lord has in store for me, but I know it's got to be better than this. I deserve better. I know God loves me and wants more for me."

KE...

"I saw my husband having sex with another man in our home. I was leaving for work and noticed a yellow motorcycle parked outside. I drove down the road, walked back to the house and wished that my husband had closed the drapes. There he was in the throes of passion, laughing with the man who rode in on the yellow motorcycle. I don't know how I got to work. All I could do was sob. My head pounded over and over in anger. I deserved to be loved like that. I deserved that passionate sex, that intimacy, and that bond. I don't know why I stay. I guess I'm hoping someday he'll actually put me and our children first."

* * *

What are our reasons for staying? Mostly it's because we're desperate to be loved and desperate to experience passion. We feel we need to continually reinvent ourselves because we're caught in the dysfunctional cycle of false expectation, disappointment, and failed outcome. We naturally fall into codependency because we want to fix everything that's out of our control. We are driven to persevere to be desired and, in doing so, become addicted to the pain of rejection. Strangely, even with all we know to be true, our heart is geared up for that pain and for that rejection; after all, the alternative is so much worse. Who wants to face shattered dreams and a broken family? Is anyone ever ready to experience that kind of loss?

Many who stay in the comfort of denial believe it's all in the name of HOPE. Yes, hope.

It's one of the most powerful words in the straight spouse dictionary.

We HOPE for change.
We HOPE for honesty.
We HOPE for communication.
We HOPE for compassion.
We HOPE that our spouse will care about us.
We HOPE that our spouse will put us first eventually.
We HOPE and HOPE and HOPE.

It's only when we realize that we may never get what we need (hoping for something impossible) that there's a painful awakening and we begin to experience the profound sadness of that reality. How do these souls survive this deep wrenching realization? Here are some answers when we posed this question and some unsolicited reports.

"My soul hasn't survived. It's dying and hanging on by a thread. There are days I just want to let go." (KW)

"I play the piano when I get the time. It reminds me of who I used to be." (Louise)

"I think I got out before my soul was consumed. That's what I've said a lot when I first joined Str8's; it felt like my soul was being sucked out of me. I haven't gotten into a peaceful or joyful thing yet, but just being in my home is giving me a sense of calm that I can't remember feeling in a long time." (Yvonne)

"My soul is still in limbo." (Dan)

"Exercise -- it clears my head and burns off frustration and stress. Journal -- it helps me process some of the emotions." (Paul)

"Oddly enough, I think my soul has come back to life. When the truth of the situation came about, it gave me a good pause to re-evaluate who I had become to survive in this drama. I looked in the mirror and saw that it wasn't me looking back anymore, and I started to reconnect with who I really am. I am writing again; prose, poetry, and even lyrics. For the first time in a long time, I'm able to express my heart's feelings and longings without being criticized for not being 'manly' enough due to my emotions and feelings. She still criticizes, but I can now see those barbs for what they are. Yes, indeed, the whole thing has sucked. But it is a good opportunity for growth and reconnecting." (Shawn)

"My soul survived. My sense of self is coming back. Some days, it was just pure determination. My blessing is my tenacity. When I am able to give to ME and reclaim things lost during my marriage, like my music, I will have completed my journey back to myself." (Leslie)

"I do try to exercise; find I miss it when I don't. Couponing is my high when I need a win. If you agree to keep faith with God and allow yourself to be led, I am sure you will find a surer footing in time." (Janet)

"In the wise words of philosopher Charles Bukowski, 'If you're losing your soul and you know it, then you've still got a soul left to lose.'" (Retrieved from http:www.goodreads.com). (Mina Beach)

"I crack jokes about my situation. I don't focus on the fact that my GH married me knowing he was gay; instead, I focus on remembering how unhappy I was most of the time with my GH and look at my newfound singlehood as a huge second chance to be happy and learn to love life again. I also pray and am grateful that TGT strengthened and renewed my relationship with the Lord. Those things have saved my soul!" (Bethany)

"In a word, FAITH. I've been carried through a great deal of challenges in my life. Sure, I've been blessed with a number of personality traits and strength, but they are just that, blessings. Holding fast to that faith by whatever means I have for learning and expressing my faith has kept my soul intact." (Loren)

"My soul took a hell of a beating. I remind myself daily to walk in this walk with humbleness and gratitude. Two months ago, I didn't know who I was. My soul was crushed. Today I am seeing reflections of my goodness from everybody I come in contact with. I notice those moments and every interaction. I don't call any of them good or bad. Slowly but surely, the soul has strength again. This journey feels long and never ending, but the truth is that we are digging down deep into an untapped source of strength that we never had to seek before. We will see the other side, and we will be there one day." (Ken)

"Some days I feel so broken and bruised. In one aspect, it does show that I am human and that there is something left in me. I'm tired of panic attacks and worry. I long for security and knowing someone will love me. I long to trust someone again. Your soul has been injured in a horrible way. It isn't 'emptied,' because you're still you. He didn't rob you of the best parts of yourself, just manipulated you into feeling this way. Let your soul heal; but please don't let him continue to have control over this more precious part of you. If you do, he wins." (Patti)

"My soul is in recovery. At least I know I have one and it hurts." (Andrea)

"Sport, exercise, singing, and being social have all helped me. These four things are something he forced me to give up. I have reclaimed them and am still finding the old me or perhaps the new and improved me." (Lori)

"A big chunk of my soul was lost to x. He took it little by little over the course of 20 years. Exercise brings me peace. During long walks, I take time out to sort out stuff in my head.

Sometimes I jog and pretend I'm running away from him and my old life. I do strength training and think of it as making my body and my own being defined and stronger." (Layla)

"When TGT first hit, I started to run every day. I also took up Tai Chi and explored other spiritual paths. I no longer run because I have a bad knee, but I do walk and have taken up yoga. I am now on a good path with my art work again (frowned upon by the Gay-X). Also, journaling the Artists Way has helped. It was a Godsend. I recommend it highly." (Marianne)

"My soul has been emptied. I have not figured out how to fill it back up again. I hope someday I can." (Wendy)

"Going to church has helped me so much. There are so many times I will end up in tears because the message has touched me so deeply. Music and exercise are also life-savers for me. It makes a world of difference in my day. Taking time to just clear my mind and think or just 'be' is also something that renews my soul. I'm guilty of not taking enough time to do that." (Martha)

"My soul is filled through my faith. So far, nothing I've encountered in life's challenges has been able to separate me from my relationship with God. No earthly man has access to my soul. Thank God!" (Lisa)

"I fell like mine is just hanging on by a thread, and I don't know what will save it from fraying yet. Right now, my family is stressing me out, so what brings me peace is when I get to leave for the weekend and snuggle with my boyfriend. I'm not finding much else that actually works right now, as I no longer am enjoying many of the things I used to. Praying something comes along to pull me out this funk I'm stuck in right now." (AK)

* * *

So, how do we break out of this last phase of the cycle that began with high expectations and unrealistic hope and now finds us facing reality with its resultant disappointment and despair? Breaking out of the cycle starts with acceptance. When we can be completely honest with ourselves, accept what our relationship really is now, and accept in our hearts and heads what might and what cannot happen, only then do we begin to figure out what we ourselves want, need, and value and to reformulate the direction of our journeys. Facing and accepting our reality takes time. Try on a pair of straight spouse shoes and walk with us through this anguishing part of our journey....

"All I ever wanted was for my husband to love me."

"I have to beg to hold hands and sit together on the couch. My wife says she's fine just sitting in the same room. It isn't the same. I need more."

"We never had romance. We were never playful. I've never known such loneliness as the day I found his cell phone. I found hundreds of texts from his boyfriend. He and his boyfriend were clearly in love. They were romantically playful and had a passion for each other. I deserve that."

"We don't have a sex life. There's no intimacy. I am so desperate to be touched, when he rolls over to go to sleep, I often have to put my arms around him just to feel close to him. He could care less."

"My ex-wife negotiated foreplay for trips to Disney. She said I put too much pressure on her when we were in the bedroom. It took her so long to have an orgasm, I'd lose my erection. Sex ended up being a challenge. I didn't have the chance to see if I could even please her because I couldn't stay hard. In the long run, I think she preferred it that way. It was a nightmare version of 'Let's Make A Deal.'"

"I've been married 22 years and have been lonely for most of my married life. My husband has never desired me. I wear lingerie, do my hair, stay in shape, and I think I look good for a woman my age. He sought a job early in our marriage that required him to travel. He was away more than he was home."

"When am I going to stop feeling sorry for myself? I can't believe this is happening. I can't stop wondering what my husband is doing when he's alone. Why do I do this to myself? Why can't I just let him go and live my life? Why am I waiting for him to let me go? Why can't I just tell him to leave? I can't tell you what the Lord has in store for me, but I know it's got to be better than this. I deserve better. I know God loves me and wants more for me."

* * *

So, again, what are our reasons for staying even when we're in this kind of pain? Mostly it is because we're desperate to be loved and desperate for passion. Who wants to face shattered dreams and a broken family? Is anyone ever ready to experience that kind of loss?

Eventually, the pain reaches the saturation level. There's only so much our souls can absorb. That's when we ask ourselves: How many more texts will I try to find? How many more spy missions will I make trying to catch her with her girlfriend? How long will I subject myself to this? How many more times will I look at him or her with love and know that it can never be reciprocated in the sexually and emotionally intimate way that I need, want and value? And, finally, looking at ourselves candidly, we ask, "How much more frustration can I myself handle?"

It's usually at this point that some of us come face to face with the fact that our spouses are simply not capable of loving us the way we need to be loved or the relationship is not good for us. Others of us realize that this marriage may not be ideal but it's not worth losing. In both cases, it becomes clear that we ourselves need to reconfigure our own identity, integrity, and belief system and use that as our new compass to guide us forward.

With this compass, we can venture into new territory. At the same time, deciding which direction is best for us requires us to pay attention to our changing feelings, thoughts, and dreams and also to pay attention to unexpected happenings that suggest new possibilities. Acting on these turning points, straight spouses move -- ever so slowly --from merely surviving toward a place where they are reconfiguring themselves in their own right as individuals -- not spouses.

Chapter 6
Turning Points

The diverse ways by which straight wives and husbands forge through the obstacles that arise after their husbands or wives come out cannot be mapped in straight lines. As they deal with the aftermath of discovery or disclosure, each spouse detours, back tracks, and sometimes circles aimlessly. Yet, for most, the direction is almost always forward, even as their individual paths gain depth and complexity.

Slowly, slowly, they understand that this newly found variable in their marriage has -- ironically enough – always been a constant. It just wasn't part of their known world until discovery or disclosure. Once they reach some level of understanding that this newly revealed constant won't change, they have a choice whether or not to change themselves to fit the new reality. Most make the choice to change and begin to make a transition in how they think, feel, breathe, and express so that they are more in tune with their new reality – even as that continues to take shape.

Yes, they create a new normal: staying married in one of many forms, separating, or divorcing. Whatever the final choice made by each spouse, all become introspective, finally able to think beyond the shock and pain and anger. It's a new challenge to detach, regain independence, and create a new identity. It takes time and patience to find their true selves. And that is the turning point, when they realize that their lives are in their own hands and there's an unfounded freedom in being there.

For readers, the overall thrust of spouses' journeys sometimes overshadows the more subtle though often more cataclysmic "turning points" that enabled each of them to move around, over, under, or through the obstacles. The following section captures some of the most common of these pivotal incidents, insights, memories, or experiences that triggered a different perception of the "reality" of a spouse's particular situation; the realization of a new angle of the "problem" they were then able to resolve constructively; or a deeper awareness of their role in the relationship tangle that motivated a change in their outlook or behavior. A turning point can be a new person, activity, or physical action that fills an unnoticed empty space in the mosaic of their lives. Focusing on just these "points" gives us a sense of the powerful trajectory of their gradual transformation.

Emma...

You get to a point where you decide that GAY is not going to define you. You get to a point where you decide that his choices are not going to define you and you won't let him take anything more from you. It certainly shaped me. I wasn't going to allow it to define me. It refined me. I got angry, and I knew that I wasn't going to let his decisions affect me anymore.

Martin...

My wife and I have been together for 20 years. We've been married for 17. When she came out, I went through the typical roller coaster: numbness, despair, anger, disbelief, and back to anger and despair. The funny thing is that, despite the emotional turmoil, our relationship is better now than before except our sex life is gone for good. We've communicated more, cried together, and hugged a lot. We've fought less. I don't hate her and am mostly over my anger. She is who she is, and I believe her when she says she didn't know she was a lesbian when we married up to the first fifteen years of our relationship. We've agreed we're destined to divorce, but we are staying married and living under the same roof until she gets her career back on track and can support herself. I'm extremely concerned about the effect of our eventual split on our kids, ages 5 and 8.

I'd reached a place of acceptance and was sure I was handling things very well, starting to get over it, fantasizing about dating again, and finding that idea pretty exciting until this morning.

I slept horribly and woke up feeling unsettled, having had an active night of dreaming – unusual because I normally sleep like the dead and don't remember dreaming at all. I made the kids breakfast and sat down to eat with them. Then, one of my dreams suddenly became very vivid. My wife and I were newlyweds We were very poor and lived in a dirty, graffiti-scarred upper flat in a bad neighborhood. We didn't have two nickels to rub together, but had each other. We were deeply in love and extremely happy. In the dream, we were in the bedroom making love on the old mattress while the stained cotton curtains flapped in the open windows. It was summer and very hot. Our bodies were glistening with sweat as they glided against each other. We made love until we collapsed in exhaustion, laughing with joy as we fell in each other's arms. In the dream, I saw everything, heard everything, smelled and tasted everything. I FELT everything just as I did when I lived it so many years ago.

The sudden memory of this dream hit me like a ton of bricks, and I broke down sobbing at the kitchen table while the kids stared at me. I cried so hard I couldn't see and couldn't talk. I had tears, snot, and drool streaming down my face. I felt like a damn fool, and the kids were confused and concerned. I'm not sure they'd ever seen me cry before. Hell, I'm crying like a baby right now just retelling the story.

So, I'm back to square one. My life is so empty, and I am so, so sad. Everything is black and I feel dead inside. I'd forgotten how good things were between us for so long and how much we loved and supported one another. I'd forgotten how happy we were with our lives and how each challenge and struggle and tragedy brought us closer together. I want my old life back! I don't WANT my children's family to be broken. I don't WANT to be divorced! I don't want to be single again! I don't WANT to start dating again! I want my wife back! I want our love back. I want us to be happy together again. And I know that will never, ever happen.

JD...

I don't know. I think I'm still moving through it. There are days I feel like I'm barely surviving and other days I have perspective.

Karen...

I am redefining myself. This is my turning point. I have to figure out what and who I am. I gave up perhaps too much of myself trying to make my marriage and family work. That's what seems weird to analyze. What am I? I thought, (and still think, due to habits) of myself as mother, wife, home-maker (since I'm a stay at home mom). Who am I? I'm Karen. I'm still trying to figure it all out and know that no matter what, being a mother is a priority. I've neglected my wants and desires for too long and have no clue who I am. I'm not the same career-driven person I was in my 20's before TGO. I can't fall back on that mind set either.

Chrissy...

I'm in Chicago for a few days. This was "home." I came here because it's time to buy a dress for my daughter's upcoming wedding. A few days ago, I was struggling with the fact I had to do this. I thought the source of my emotions was due to all that had changed in my life. We're a different family now and there's no changing all that's happened.

Even though I thought I'd dealt with all the changes, something still was making me dread getting on the plane to get here. I thought having to deal with the ex on a few things might be the reason. While I knew it would be unpleasant, that knowledge still did not change how I was feeling. It took a lot to get on the plane and keep my emotions in check. Yesterday was a whirlwind day so I didn't have a chance to really deal with what was bothering me.

Today I know what it was. I've been dreading coming home because I thought it would be too painful to see all the things I had to change in my life because of decisions that were made which were not of my choice. I was afraid I'd never be able to come home and never be able to feel settled in my new life in California that I also love so very much.

So I went out and drove by old familiar places: my house, the kids' schools, the football field where my son played ball, shops, the forest and camps, and the old coffee shop where the guy made the coffee "just right." And what I found out was that I'm fine. I'm really ok with it. I needed to come here and deal with all of these things. I needed to give myself permission to either cry or celebrate "I made it!" I have made it, and there were no tears, just a sense of peace.

It's time now. It's time to let go of all the things that keep me from that last tiny step in my forward journey. I am ready. I am happy. I know I have made it to the other side.

Reginald (UK)...

I've been on this roller-coaster since February when my soon-to-be-ex-wife told me that there was someone else. She told me she had a female family friend from the USA we had known since before the children were born. I was blindsided. I have three children: 2 boys, 13 and 7, and a princess, aged 9. The children live with me in the family house. My soon-to-be-ex moved to a flat which was rented by her new "chosen life partner." The children don't know this and have no idea that "Auntie" is on the scene. They only know they get expensive gifts now and then from her and that Mummy has taken holiday to the states quite a bit.

I went through a period of profound shock and depression. Eventually, I found a straight spouse online mailing list and lurked for a while before throwing myself into a posting (sometimes at drunken desperate times). At all times, I've been cared for there. I've been treated as I realize I am a cared-for familee member who is strong for you when you can't be strong for yourself. This online group helped me get through the worst emotional time of my life and became an important part of my recovery. I'd exhausted my friends in real life, but now am able to enjoy their company. I returned to church after an absence of 20 years. I am getting on with my studies and have even been on a couple dates.

Just when I think I see the light at the end of the tunnel, I tunnel back to bad places. Maybe I don't like the fact she is getting on with her life. It may be that I feel she owes me something or owes me an explanation. I know in my heart it is never going to happen. I just don't want my stomach to churn at the news that she is living a normal life whilst mine is in ruins. I have to remind myself my life is NOT in ruins. I spend too much time thinking, "If I was the me I am now with her as she was...." I don't want to argue with myself anymore. I don't want that. How do I tell myself that?

Sally...

Transitioning is surely a process. It remains as unique and common as this whole experience is for all of us. Are there stages? There probably are. I know for me the "triggers" didn't cause such roller coasters for me. I know that I realized I'd stopped seeing my choices and actions through his eyes and ways he would react. I stopped using him in my mind as the one with the power to deem my choices as achievement or failure. I became my own guide. In the "transition" stage, TGT is no longer a daily struggle nor a daily event. For me, transitioning really turned out to be transitioning into the life I took full responsibility for. It meant realizing I was whole.

JS...

For me it was anger. I absolutely boiled over with it, seething and yelling. Never in my life have I been so angry at someone. Once anger took over as my dominant emotion, I was able to leave. Before that I was stuck in depression and could barely function, let alone get my life back in order.

C…

The defining moment early on for me was when my best str8 friend encouraged me to move out of the shared bedroom. It was not only a necessary step for me, but also a vindication of sorts. My ex was completely caught off guard that I had mustered ANY will power to create boundaries. It just got better and better from that point.

Loren…

Looking back, I had at least four transition moments. I wouldn't say that all of them went from survival to moving forward, but I'd say that each of them completely changed my overall goal and prompted me to take a new turn from what I was doing before that moment.

The first transition was when I decided not to approach my GIDH for anything sexual again. It not only created the first of many boundaries but also allowed me to see all the other ways he was abusive, layer by layer. I began a long road of boundary creation to stop his verbal daggers from sinking in. My goal was to stick with the marriage and simply not let his abuse do any further harm.

The second transition was when I told myself that boundaries weren't enough and that I needed to get out of my marriage. I began to work on not just resisting his damage, but gaining the strength to take a stand. My goal was to actually believe that I could make it on my own.

The third transition was when I uttered the words, "I need to divorce you because you are gay (among other things)." I told some family and friends, too, which meant there was no turning back. My goal was to move forward with divorce and not let him change my mind.

The fourth transition was 13 months after my divorce when I bought my house. It was when I started to build a new life without him.

KR...

Have I transitioned? I really pondered this. The answer is "yes." I didn't have an epiphany moment or anything dramatic. I just realized that I don't love him anymore as a spouse. I don't hate him anymore either. Distance is the biggest help. I have a good plan to get my life on track, and it seems to be working. We will still be married for a while due to health insurance. TGO and I aren't adversaries, so we're able to spend our time building our separate futures instead of wasting it on tearing each other apart. I am very lucky with that and I hope it continues.

EK...

I am really trying to move on with a new life, but I feel like I'm sputter-starting. Parts of days feel good, but big parts leave me feeling either overwhelmed or agitated. I've never been alone in my whole life! Thank God for the dogs!

Terry...

A child is one of the greatest gifts God can give, and I thought maybe having children would change our situation. One evening, I popped the question, and she agreed. It was really more like a business deal. Nine months later, my son was born. The first time he looked at me he had a portion of my heart for life. It still puts a tear into my eyes just thinking about this blessed event.

The marriage did improve, but not for long, so I thought to ask for a divorce. My friends told me that indecisiveness is normal and I should stick it out for my children, which I did. Was I happy with that decision? Yes, for my boys' sake, but I was unhappy with me. So, I thought maybe another child is all we needed to get things going again. I thought maybe a bigger family would open for us the flood gates again. Nine months later, my younger son was born. I was now the richest man in the world because of my two beautiful boys.

Life went on. One night, for no apparent reason, I asked her if she was committing adultery. She said no, but my sixth sense didn't believe her. I'd always trusted my gut feeling and this time I was going to listen. I started to read books on what to look for when someone is going to cheat on you. She had all of the characteristics stated in the books.

In my twelfth year of marriage, she started to distance further. In November, when I tried to kiss her while we were having sex, she turned her head the other way and started to shed a tear. I asked her once more if she was committing adultery and added the question, "Is it with a man or a woman?" My sixth sense told me to do so.

She looked stunned, but said, "No." The way she said it, I knew she was lying.

On our fifteenth anniversary, we went to Manhattan, where we'd spent our honeymoon. I tried to make it "special," but she was having these blank stares for no reason. The episodes were becoming more and more frequent. Not long after, I was on a business trip to Chicago. I phoned her every day to see how she was doing and to tell her that I loved her. She tried to make our conversations shorter and shorter. Her voice reminded me of a school girl in love. It was higher and more feminine. I knew I was in trouble and had to prepare for the worst at home.

For three months, it was a living hell. She was always leaving to get groceries or needing to run other emergency errands. She was wearing makeup and perfume in copious amounts, which she rarely did for me now, so I knew she was cheating. She was distancing at a rapid rate. The marriage was being dissolved through the cracks. Can you imagine, even on my birthday, she cried after we made love?

When I drove her and the boys to the airport for a visit to her parents, I kissed her to wish her a safe trip. Her kiss back was the coldest I'd ever received from anyone. It was without any soul. While they were away, I met up with a good friend for coffee and told him about my situation. He reconfirmed by suspicions; she was having an affair. But I needed proof. He told me about software that enables you to find any password on any computer. She had for a long time placed a password on her email because her university professor told her to do so. I was in post-secondary education for four years and none of my teachers ever told me to do that. I tried a trial version of the software, and let it perform its magic. Those 10 seconds letting it find the password were the longest of my life. Then, all of a sudden, I got the password, typed it in, and started to look at her emails, one by one. It ripped my heart out in a million pieces. The passion I was looking for was given to someone else. I never heard words ever from her mouth like the ones she used talking to her lover.

The more I read, the angrier I got. I got a name and looked into the yellow pages and went on websites to find out who this person was so we could have a "Gentleman's Chat." Then I found a secret folder with her lover's pictures. My heart stopped beating for a minute; then I went into shock. It was not a man, but a woman!

I phoned my wife and confronted her. A few days later, I went to pick her and the boys up at the airport. How could I see her again? She lied all these years; what am I supposed to do? Then I saw her coming towards me and knew by her expression that my marriage was dead. Two days later, she asked for a divorce and said she was moving to her partner's. The lines in the sand were drawn; the battle was set. But how can I fight when the winds were taken out of my sails?

For a month and a half, I cried twenty-four hours a day, seven days a week. She still lived under the same roof, but, adding fuel to the fire, her partner was phoning up with no consideration for me. I hate to say it, but my son was the man of the house till I could gather myself together. I asked her why she did this to me. She didn't have an answer. Some comments were plain evil. Can you imagine someone telling you it was your behavior that turned her into a lesbian?

With all this emotional baggage, I had to find a way out, and the easiest was to take my life. I tried twice but to anyone who says that they don't have a guardian angel watching over them, I have evidence to the contrary. The first time, I drove two and a half times over the posted speed limit into a major highway. Can you believe that my car did a 72 degree slide and there were no cars on a Friday night? Go figure.

At a low point, I tried numerous counselors. The problem is when you tell them what happened, their responses are less than favorable. As a last resort, I phoned the local Gay and Lesbian Association and they directed me to the Straight Spouse Network. It was a Godsend. I found out that I was not alone in this journey. It's here where I've met a very special person who has had an incredible impact on my life.

Helen…

For me it was forgiveness. On Yom Kippur, I saw him and told him I forgave him. It was like a weight had been lifted from my shoulders and I felt like I could move on. Another key moment for me was when I gave him away at his commitment ceremony. Once I did that, I didn't feel "tied" to him anymore.

Eric…

Today is the one week marker. We've been together thirteen years and have three children, ages 3, 5, and 8. We lived a Christian life. She became very fundamental, believing that if she was a good daughter to God, he'd take her pains away. She prayed fervently and played the part of the good Christian wife. Our sex life was fantastic, at least for me. She kind of considered it a "ministry," as my drive was daily or better.

While she enjoyed it to a degree and the biology worked many times for her, she wasn't able to connect emotionally with me during sex. We attributed this to the pains of her past, but I really never understood how much if affected her. She gave a great show, one even she believed for years.

Her homosexual thoughts consumed her. She'd cry, repent, and then slip into shame. This cycle was near daily, tearing her apart. Six months ago, she cast off Christianity. This gave her freedom morally to decide what was next. She couldn't ignore her desires anymore and approached the idea of being "bisexual" or "open," but we never acted on it. Two weeks ago, while I was away on work, the shame became too much. She devalued her life to the point that it was more of a burden on the world than a benefit and, without a hell to be afraid of, death was the best option. She then weighed what would be more shameful for the children and me: a wife/mom that committed suicide or one that was gay. She chose suicide.

Thank God, her friend figured out what was happening and flew up to be with her. If she'd not arrived, my poor wife would be gone. But that leads to another choice. Since death isn't the answer, she told me last week she is gay and our relationship is over. She doesn't have a love interest and isn't looking forward to finding one. It's simply the release of pressure from having to give herself to me physically and the ability to acknowledge her own thoughts and desires.

We'll make it. We're not going to be the same, and I'm broken hearted. I've never sobbed as an adult, but find myself doing it quite often. It would have almost been easier if she'd cheated. I could hate her and try to punish her. Most importantly, I believe she is a good person and cares for me and the children. This isn't something she made up, and it isn't something that can be cured with counseling or a pill. This was a last resort, where she had two choices. I'd rather have her as gay than dead.

Roger…

My wife and I had the best marriage. It was a 90% marriage: 90% of the time it was wonderful and 10% it sucked! After disclosure, my wife says the marriage was 60/40 or 50/50. The bad 50% was due to the sex issue, and the other 50% was just issues that I needed to fix and I am.

On April 11, my wife came home about 4:30 am from a party. She passed out and her cell phone went off. I picked it up and saw a message from her friend (girlfriend) saying she hoped she'd gotten home okay. The text closed, "Love you." This was a surprise. From there, I went digging back in the texts and found more information. That's when I lost it! When I checked her email, the full weight of what was going on hit me. There was so much talk about love, wants, and crap like that I was just devastated.

Later that day, I asked the wife if she'd seen the girlfriend the night before. She said no. The next few days are a blur. They were filled with much crying and hurt and sitting at work, incapacitated. This changed five days later. I talked to my sister-in-law, who said that my wife had told her the night before that she thought she was a lesbian. The lights went off. There it was.

This was the first time she'd lied to me, and it was devastating. All that crap with sex and intimacy that I had dealt with for almost six years made sense. It was not me. No matter what I could do to change, to fix all the bad things, to create new things, nothing I could do would ever make me a woman. This was not my fault. Looking back, this realization was a huge milestone.

Rafe…

Well, I just watched the gay wife and the kids leave for their camping trip. I had to review everything camper-related with her as she has never towed our 30-foot trailer nor has she ever set it up. That's always been my job. I couldn't stop hugging the boys. I just sat with them and held them a while. I didn't let them see me cry. I know they'll have fun, but I didn't want them to go. They kept asking me to take more days off work and come with them. I told them things were too busy after our last vacation and my boss needed me here. That was a half-truth.

I know once I settle down, I'll enjoy this time alone until Saturday afternoon. But it was really hard to see them go. I'm a bit of a mess right now. I kind of feel like the train hit me again. I guess there will be a lot of "firsts" that I'll need to get used to.

Lisa Michelle Smith…

I know that I have received an abundance of gifts from God. What I don't know is how to shake the melancholy that creeps around and whispers in my ear so softly that I can't figure out what it's trying to tell me. Perhaps it's just the anticipation that this time of year brings, along with the mistaken notion that my family is incomplete. I know I am where I'm supposed to be. Liking it is just taking some work.

(Later, Lisa shared an event on an online support group chat forum. This is her post.)

Well, this will be a day to go down in the historical book of Lisa's life. After 2+ years past disclosure, my GH is "officially" gay. He had not been with another man intimately until tonight. Honestly, I've needed this to happen to get some closure. But, I am also shaken by the confirmation. I guess the wound wasn't completely healed yet.

(These are the replies to the post.)

((((Hugs Lisa)))) Although we already "know" they're gay, that final confirmation still hurts. Like Jim said, another step forward in this journey. Thinking of you. (Lori)

((((hugs))))) I'm glad you have your disclosure. I wish for it, but suspect I'd feel conflicted by reality. Moving forward. (Holly)

(((Lisa))) Did he tell you this? How terribly painful, but I hope it does bring you more closure from this confirmation. Many hugs!!! (LR)

Hugs (((Lisa)))) Yes, although you knew, it is still hard to hear it being confirmed. Take care of that wound. We are out here with the balm if you are needing more. (Kathryn)

Buzz...

It's been almost four months since the ex-gay wife moved out. I've been coping pretty well after two weeks of not seeing my daughter and baby son. I had them with me today, and I have been an emotional wreck. I found a photo of my daughter. She was about two and half. She was playing in a maze we stopped at on our way back from a holiday in the snow. This sent me into a spiral of emotions, and I'm not coping well. All day, the memory from that one photo kept popping into my head. I was fighting back tears even while my daughter was with me. The problem isn't the loss of my in-denial gay ex-wife, it's the loss of my family. I look at that picture and remember how happy we were. It was a wonderful day. We all had a lot of fun. We were a family.

I don't have a family anymore, and I'm feeling it most keenly right now. I agreed to take every second weekend with my daughter, but it isn't working. I'm not handling being away from her for so long, and I'm worried about the effect it's having on my 6-month-old son who barely recognized me this morning.

In addition, I had to deal with the ex-gay wife showing me pictures this morning of her taking the kids to the beach and parks and meeting up with friends with kids. How can I compete with that? I have two days to her twelve in which to make as much of an impression as possible with my daughter, and I can't give her those memories. I don't have many friends with children her age nor the time to spend properly with her.

Intellectually, I know separating was the right thing to do, but my heart is not believing me anymore. I see ex-wife living well, getting money out of me, spending time with the kids, being part of a family, and here I am on the outside, desperately wanting my family back.

Despite the negative things about our relationship, I'm almost tempted to try to reconcile just to regain that family feeling.

RL...

I think my defining moment was about two years post divorce when I no longer cried day and night, adjusting to the visitation schedule when my son was away from me. He was just 4. I couldn't move on emotionally until I knew all his needs were met. Like many, I divorced in the anger stage of grieving. I got a lot done relatively quickly. I had a lot of focus. I seemed to be most productive when angry. But the fall out is a whole other issue. I think my defining moment was when I realized that I had established a new life and it was comfortable. I was in a whole new routine, and my life was no longer about him, but about me. He crops up only now and then which is exactly the way I like it.

Mary Francis...

Time and distance are the two things that helped most in the transformation. Emotional distance, mental distance, and physical distance worked together to get me through survival mode and into moving forward. Filing for divorce separated me from his choices and actions (and inactions) so I could start to focus on my life instead of his or ours. Moving into my own place -- a place he never set foot in -- was physical separation that gave a boost to my sense of having my own life. Becoming legally divorced set me free to truly get on with my life.

Carolyn...

The first transition for me was while I was still married but had outed him. We were still in joint counseling, trying to figure out what we should do. This was about four months into TGT. I had initially had two reactions: one, it wasn't me; two, what was different? We had lived as brother and sister for years and years and years.

Our joint therapist kept asking me what I wanted. (Gee, sound like Amity much?) I didn't have a clue. I had never put my own needs first EVER. I was at a real loss.

To make matters worse, I found out about yet another instance in which he'd put our finances, my credit rating, AND my security clearance in jeopardy. I burst into tears, which says a great deal because my meds don't let me cry for sad things. I said, "Definitively, I know what I want! I want to feel loved, honored, and cherished the way I've done for him for 32 years." He responded honestly, "I don't think I can do that." And I responded honestly, "Then I want out. I want a divorce."

The second transition was when he actually moved out which was four months after the decision and eight months into TGT.

The third transition was a combination of HUGE things on the stress scale: new condo, new car, retired from 33 years of government service, visiting other str8s, traveling to family in upstate NY and London, UK. I overwhelmed myself.

The fourth transition was when I finally told him in an email that I didn't want to hear from him again nor see him again and that I was tired of him using me as his caretaker whenever he had a major life crisis. I told him it sent me into downward spirals I couldn't handle. This worked. I haven't heard from him nor spoken to him in years now.

I don't think I've really moved to a new life, though, as sad as that is. I do what I can when I can, but my health is an impediment.

* * *

The experiences that these voices describe so vividly as their turning points are "aha" moments that somehow bring about a shift in straight spouses' thinking. Whether slight or huge, the shift enables them to make concrete decisions for themselves, by themselves, and gives them the tenacity needed to take that first baby step forward no matter how small. They finally have clarity, key to seeing who they are.

Having forged through the fire, they being to forgive themselves and love themselves enough to be willing and determined to discern the best route to move forward as difficult as that might be. First, however, there are still dilemmas to be resolved and choices to be made. Yes, it can become an exhausting tug of war between this or that, now or later, here or there.

Chapter 7
Tug of War

The line in the sand is drawn. The white flag is knotted and hanging over neutral ground, waiting. Opposing forces are pulling at couples as they dig in their heels and try to figure out if they should remain married or if they should separate. Like every marriage, every game of tug of war is unique, yet the teams seem to look the same. On one side, there's fear, guilt, anxiety, anger, selfishness, and grief; and, on the other, there's hope, risk, courage, determination, empathy, and faith. On one sideline, waiting to play in the game are denial, narcissism, panic, disgust, self-loathing, and pity. On the other sideline are sympathy, affection, understanding, and unconditional love.

Many couples desire to work through every possible scenario to figure out if anything will work for them, from swinging to polyamory to an open marriage to celibacy; others determine it's better to detach and let go. What works for one pair may not for another, and, whatever they decide, there's pure exhaustion in the process. The governing question for each partner is "How do you know if or when you should just let go?"

One straight wife on the WOBGH, (Wives of Bi/Gay Husbands mailing list), offered to her fellow list members the strategy of starting with a picture of their marriages before determining if they should stay or go. "See if our needs are met," she suggested, "and determine if they can be." She also advised making a list and answering some very tough questions. "Write everything down you need and want in your marriage on the left hand column and check off what you really have on the right. The most important advice is NOT to check off what you bargain for, what you nag for, or have to cue, prompt and remind him to do. If you do it honestly, it should give you a real glance at where life is for you now."

She then shared her own list:

"I need/want:
Honesty
Commitment
Trust
Communication
Fidelity
Intimacy
A sex life
For him to initiate sex
To be desired/wanted
To be loved
To feel secure
Laughter-Joy
Emotional support
Help with the kids
Help with the house
Him to get a job
To have fun with my husband
Him to be home on time
A good provider-to provide financial stability
Insurance/medical coverage for me/children
Our business/company to survive
For him to be the spiritual head of our home."

She also asked herself questions, which she shared with list members:

"Do you trust your spouse?
Do you trust your own emotions and insights?
Do you and your husband engage in honest, open communication?

Is there intimacy, romance, and genuine desire?
Do you worry or obsess about what your spouse is doing, spending countless hours wondering where your spouse is?
Do you find you're anxious because you suspect and want proof?
Did you buy spyware or anything else to help you validate what you already know?
Do you feel connected or isolated in your marriage?
Do you feel like a roommate?
Does your spouse do anything to foster the love between you?
Does your spouse edify you, emotionally support you, and care for your well being?
Do you spend a lot of time and energy in doubt, mistrust, and lamenting over what you're missing?"

Are spouses startled when they read what they listed? Are they surprised by their answers to these questions? Some are; some aren't. The more honest their answers are, the closer the individuals are to acceptance. The bottom line questions, in any case, are: Are your needs being met? Do you think they can be?

Each spouse knows only what he or she knows. Yet, it's hard to figure out what one's needs are. A wife who tried this process wrote, "I'm disgusted. I look at how many years I've spent worrying, obsessing and tracking, trying to solve his issues when he could care less about mine. I finally realized that I need to start focusing all that energy into me, my children and my future."

One spouse may decide he or she needs monogamy; another may need an open marriage; and yet another needs to separate. If a couple decides to step forward together, solving the delicate puzzle requires 100% commitment from both the straight and the gay, lesbian, bisexual, or trans spouse. To break out of their perceptions of marriage and redefine what it means to them, both spouses practice open and honest communication. As one still-married straight husband on several mailing lists writes in his standard reply to fellow spouses who want to stay married, "COMMUNICATE, COMMUNICATE, COMMUNICATE." Honest communication leads to making new rules and maybe each spouse's sacrificing some needs. Constant redefining and stepping forward on the redefined path are the ways they find out what, if anything, will work.

Whether spouses decide to stay or go, they then face more choices that pull them this way and that. Two major needs emerge, and meeting each of them makes it possible to move forward on their post-disclosure journeys. One need is to detach or let go from what they had or thought they had. The other is the need to bring closure to the life they had lived up to that point.

To detach, one spouse asked herself, "How are you letting go? What emotional habits have you given yourself permission to stop doing for your spouse? What are you no longer taking accountability for emotionally? What are you no longer physically doing that you may have done just last week? Last month? What are you doing for you?"

Another wife, when asked, "How did you detach?" explained on an online support list, "You'll gain some emotional control if you detach. It is like nothing I have felt for a long time. This will be especially hard for those of you who still adore your husband. I recently had a traumatic experience that turned those feelings upside down for me, so it has helped me detach. I still feel sad and it's painful to think of what I have to do, but, for some reason, I feel that because I value my own existence more, his behavior seems unbearable. A few things that started to change in me and might for you were:

"You'll stop the brain damage that comes from searching for proof. You probably already know enough to end the marriage.

"You'll stop thinking you can change him. You can only change you. You will start to process the fact that 'you can't fix him.'

"You'll reignite parts of yourself that don't include him, and you'll find parts of yourself that bring you joy, so you have some part of you that doesn't involve him.

"Over time, you will start to look at him and his behavior and make him own it. You no longer make excuses for him and his choices. You start taking responsibility only for you.

"You'll build your support system to help YOU. He is not part of your support system. He can't even figure out who he is much less how to deal with your needs or feelings. You need to find women (or men who don't want to bang you) who will unconditionally love and support you without judgment. This online site is the perfect place to start. You have already begun if you signed up here.

"If you have children, take the energy, love, creativity, and spirituality you were giving to him and give it to them. They deserve and need it. You're building grownups. He is responsible for his own relationship with them, and you, yours. I am not saying be a helicopter mom and hover and smother, but give them the love that has not been accepted by him in the ways they need it individually. If you don't have children, give it to some other deserving person who can actually give pure love back."

Specific ways by which spouses detach from their husbands or wives are as diverse as they are themselves…

"For me the big one was to stop asking, 'How are you doing?' Processing emotions was a big thing we did together. We both put a lot of energy into that. Once I pulled myself out of that part of the relationship, distancing happened relatively smoothly, even though we stayed in the same bed without sex for 8 months." (Bart)

"Maybe it was just as much about me. The more I put my needs first, the more I could let him go, I rediscovered myself, loved myself and put me first. Then I was able to love and be loved by someone else!" (Delilah)

"After a while, I stopped reassuring him that he wasn't a bad person. I guess I realized I was trying to take care of him, but I realized he could do that. I can't be the mom to everyone. I also have to take care of me." (AL)

"I detached when I realized that no matter how I changed and what I did, he would never love me. Up until that point, I fought hard at a losing battle for a marriage that just wasn't meant to be. It's hard to love someone who cannot and will not return that love. I realize that now. And, although it's hard, I am taking steps to move on and for the first time in a very long time, I am happy." (TLB)

One thing I think it helpful is to change your inner and outer language to start expressing your thoughts in terms of "I" instead of "we." When you notice a "we" thought, change it to an "I" thought. With a little practice, you do see your attitude shifting. (Tom)

What was the breaking point? When he broke the last promise he ever made. I knew I would never receive the love I needed nor would he keep the commitment he made at the altar. I realized all my efforts were in vain. I had to face the reality that no matter what I did, he would never be faithful. That's when I let go legally. (RL)

* * *

If couples divorce or physically separate, detachment becomes easier, some say inevitable. For those who stay together, the most difficult aspects of detaching are, first, breaking down old perceptions, expectations, routines, and habits that they had before this new information entered their lives and then reconfiguring themselves to create the persons they want to become.

Separated, divorced, or still married, however, all spouses need closure from the life that was if they want to begin anew. Different from detachment, closure is filling that terrible, nagging need to be validated. How do they get that validation of closure? Surprisingly, it doesn't come from the LGBT spouse. Ultimately, it comes from the straight spouses' own ability to forgive themselves and others.

Even if their partners disclosed and even when spouses have concrete proof, there's still a degree of darkness in their lives as they try to piece together the details. Disclosure and evidence alone don't always bring closure because there are too many unanswered questions blocking the way to the whole truth. Yes, the unknown comes into view, but it can be a very dim view. Rather than immediate clarity and relief, there's heartache.

Spouses look back on every vacation, every day off their wives or husbands said they had taken, every business trip, every late night. Curiosity is unquenched, leading often to feeling even more insecure as they wonder, "When did she really know?" "Has he been acting the whole time?" "Did she really love me and my children?" "Was my whole marriage a lie?" "Why the hell didn't I see this coming?"

The tug of war between closure and unanswered questions persists for a long time. Listen to the turmoil it can cause...

"Isn't it ironic that it took my marriage to learn that there's intense physical pain when you suffer deep emotional loss? I can't describe the loneliness and despair of wanting to be wanted. It was here in this emotional place that I had also asked for a divorce but hadn't yet filed. It was a Saturday morning before our son was awake. We were having coffee and Max said, 'How about a shower? Let's try for number two before Jordan wakes up.' I had to summon every bit of strength to be aloof. I calmly said, 'Go ahead. I'm going to finish my coffee and read the paper.' I looked up only once. He left with tears in his eyes. He knew I had nothing left to give. I felt a great sense of closure from this chapter in my life. It was just a matter of time before I could start a life of my own." (RL)

"I thought by moving out I'd have closure. My wife came out and is living with her girlfriend in our home. My children don't live with me anymore; they now visit. Sure, I know she's gay and that's part of it. What kills me is living every day knowing she lied to me and was unfaithful. How do you trust someone ever again? It will haunt me the rest of my life." (FR)

"I thought if only I was a better wife I could possibly win my husband's love back. I did everything to make our marriage work and was totally losing myself. He continued to lie and deceive me, hooking up with men on Craig's List. I filed for divorce last October, and it was final on September 19th of this year. It was just a month short of what would have been our 25th Anniversary. I choose to have little or no contact with him. I find with no contact comes no confusion. I am trying to rebuild my life without him. I often feel sad, angry, and a whole range of emotions, but I know that is all part of the loss and of finally letting go. I hope we all end up in a better place eventually. I could have never made it this far without finding SSN. Thanks to all of you who helped me along the way." (JM)

"I moved on. My husband came out. I filed for divorce. It took time for him to find a place of his own. I met the love of my life, and now we have kids of our own in addition to mine. Closure takes time. It happens when you are no longer interested in anything your spouse is doing. It happens when your life is all about you." (HH)

"I found closure by doing the things I love to do. I hike, travel, and I love to bike. The early days were the worst. Once time passes and you adjust to divorced life, you learn to live your life for you. No one else will." (Anon)

"I don't have closure. My wife came out, but she never apologized for anything. She destroyed our family. She never put our daughter or our family first. The only thing that mattered was her girlfriend and her new life. I don't think she'll ever own up to what she's done. I don't think she can. I look at old pictures of the way things used to be and just cry." (JD)

"I don't know if I'll ever get closure. My husband came out; we live together still. We have a business and can't divorce. It's hell. Every day, I have to look at him. I can't stop wondering how long he'd been unfaithful. He said it was only in the last two years. I don't believe him. I've at least gotten to a place where I only focus on me." (EA)

* * *

In the end, the core questions are: Do I stay or go? Can I let go emotionally from what was? Can I forgive myself? Others? If I do let go and find some level of closure, what in life might be waiting and what hole might never be filled, hard as I want that to happen? One such chasm remains after more than ten years for Duane, "veteran" straight spouse, active in supporting other straight spouses and working for LBGT equality. As he explains, "While the pain would have still been deep, I would have preferred she hurt me honestly than to kill me with her lies. The only regret that I can honestly say I have is that I have lost my belief in love. While I have so much love bottled up inside of me, I don't know if I will ever truly be able to openly give my heart and trust to another." (Buxton, 2012).

Despite profound losses, most spouses eventually detach and determine closure to some degree, whether or not they stay married. How to do so is a perennial question that hounds them all. Answering it requires each one to select what pieces of himself or herself to keep, which to change, and which to jettison and then to determine what gaps need filling.

All this happens as they move from surviving to thriving. Many have done so. Many more will.

Chapter 8
Now

"Now" is a word that suggests transition and impermanence, a past "left behind" and a future that will change things. For straight spouses, however, their sense of "now" is how they measure how far along they have progressed in their journeys, comparing who they once were to the persons they are becoming and long to be. Most important, their sense of "who I am now" becomes clearer the longer they work on rediscovering and reconfiguring their needs, wants, and values.

To give you a sense of this cumulative experience that keeps redefining "now," we conclude this book with two stories. One is the full-fledged saga of a woman's painful and powerful transformation, and the other is an abbreviated but strong declaration of where a man found himself seven years after his lesbian wife came out.

We first introduce Evangeline, who is still married yet has defined a life for herself that is uniquely her own. Then Carlos shares his public statement, the rhetoric of which encapsulates his present sense of who he is and also affords us glimpses between the lines into his emotional upheaval and heartache as he forged his way to his "now."

Evangeline is one of the spouses who was able to detach, come to closure, reconfigure, and transform her life. Her story falls into distinctive chapters.

In a Nutshell

God is my cornerstone and I'll tell you about Father Martin later. What's most important about him right now is the homily he gave on Sunday. He started by telling us about how African hunters trap monkeys. Hunters hollow out a coconut and cut it in half. They cut a hole in one half of the shell just barely big enough to fit a monkey's hand. They put a very ripe orange in the other half of the shell and fasten the two halves together. Using rope, they hang this contraption from a tree and wait. An unsuspecting monkey looking for a delicious snack smells the orange and realizes it's inside the coconut. It reaches inside for the orange and grabs it voraciously, trying to pull it through the hole. While the monkey is distracted, hunters throw a net over it and capture it. Had the monkey realized all he had to do was let go of the orange, it could have saved its own life. I've been thinking a lot lately about that orange.

I have started my story many times, but it did not make sense to me because I kept forgetting that I needed to tell you who and what I am. I am a Louisiana Creole. That means my heritage is of many peoples. In my case, I'm African, French, Chinese, and Native American. We are a people of oral stories and deep traditions. Catholicism is our religion, but it means so much more to us than religion. It is every breath we take to sustain our physical being and our spiritual soul. I am a descendent of many strong women who always kept God first in their hearts, and the importance of family guided them to make decisions.

A few women of my past. Marie-Therese was born into slavery in the 1740's, gained her freedom, secured the freedom of her children, and, by the time of her death, was one of the largest land owners in Central Louisiana. Odette—her husband died leaving her with four small children to protect from a greedy and cruel brother-in-law. Suzanne, also a widow and with 13 children, had to hold two family businesses together during the Great Depression. And my mother, Josephine, whom doctors told not to have any children due to a medical condition, who brought five healthy children into this world. Over the past 270 years, these women would light a candle in the night and pray to God to guide them to do what was best for their family no matter what cost to them as women.

What am I? I am a woman that lives in the 21st century, but every beat of my heart is that of the women of my cultural past. For the past 25 years, I've been hard on myself. Why did I stay in this marriage for 25 years after disclosure? How weak am I? Before I started writing my story, I had decided to back to counseling to try to get answers to these questions, but now I understand. For me to have made any other choice would have gone against everything I am. I do not suggest that any sane person make the decisions I made, and I hope this story does not sound like I am making excuses. I know that the most another person can do to you is to give you a bad situation and it is your choice how you respond. On judgment day, it will only be me and God and I cannot point fingers at my husband and say, "You did this to me."

I don't know where to start. In 1974, girl met nice boy and they fell in love. In 1976, she marries nice boy and they have two beautiful children. In 1986, one day after our daughter's fifth birthday, four days before our tenth wedding anniversary and 14 days before my 31st birthday, my husband told me he had something he needed to share with me. He needed to be tested for AIDS because he'd slept with men! My world as I knew and understood it ended.

I went into shock. I prayed to God to guide me and tell me what was best for our children, Jean-Paul, 8, and Desiree, 5. Raul and I went to counseling, but as I looked back on the first ten years of our marriage, I saw the deceit from the start, like when he invited his fraternity brother with his wife and kids to spend vacations with us in our home. It was only later that I found out they were lovers. I felt he'd betrayed me on the day he said, "I do." Neither Raul nor I wanted to share his secret. How little did I know that he was pulling me into his closet and one day he would walk out and leave me there?

Looking back, I made two big mistakes. The biggest one was that I got angry with God. This is when I fell away from the strong women of my past and culture. The second was not sharing with my family. I've been blessed with a family that supports me no matter what happens. When I made the decision to stay, a decision I thought that was best for my family, I ended up turning my back on God and the support of my family. I see now that it was my pride. I thought to myself, "Evangeline cannot have a broken marriage." So, for 19 years I did not tell a soul.

Who's my husband? Well, he's a man who's always done what he thinks society has wanted him to do. He came from a Southern Baptist family and told me he would go to church praying that God would take "gay" away. He beats up on himself a lot. He has a lot of guilt battling his need for a man and the commitment he made to me at the altar. My heart goes out to him. It was most evident after our first born son arrived; I felt he was almost disappointed in me. When I look back on it, I feel he thought that if he played by all the rules, got married, and had children, he would feel joy. He's never been completely fulfilled with our family. It's never been enough.

I do believe he married me because he truly loved me in his own way. I believe his heart was with me. I look back on the intimate sexual side of our marriage. It confuses me because we were very compatible. I could not have wanted nor asked for a better lover. He would tell me that he could lose himself in me, and, at those very intimate moments, he said he felt we were as one and that he felt complete. I think this is one of the reasons it was so hard for me to give him up. He was fighting a demon. Raul wants to be that man of character, and I know he had fought gay before we were ever married. The innate desire for the same-sex attraction is stronger than that which we can control.

Best Actress

From 1986 to 2000, we moved a lot. I think we were running. Raul was an officer in the Army. He gave up his commission, and we went back home to Louisiana to be closer to family. It was hard, but we kept the secrets and then moved to Florida. Our children grew strong and healthy. Our family life brought me joy. We did everything together. If you knew us, we looked like the perfect couple. I continued the way most people knew me before disclosure: I was always laughing and the life of the party. But, over the years, I became tired and the laughter was no longer from my heart. When we would have dinner parties, I would always hug the last guest a little longer. What I was saying in my heart, "Don't go. Don't leave me here in this nightmare." Every year when Hollywood would give the Best Actress award for the Oscar, I would whisper to myself, "No, she is only second best."

Enslavement

By 2000, the kids grew up, moved away, and Raul did, too, emotionally and physically. He was never home. When he met Larry, who became his lover, the hardcore pain started. I felt like a widow. No one knew about it, so no one came to console me. Every time I'd see him, it was like the man I'd married was dead and someone had taken over his body. It was that way for about fourteen years. He was constantly coming and going, trying to find himself, and I was letting him do it, thinking he would come back to me. I did tell someone that I felt foolish. I married with my heart and loved with my soul. If that's foolishness, I am guilty as charged. Why did I stay?

I was happy to be at work. It was the only time I could really forget the pain. The minute the day was over, I'd dread the thought of going home. I dreaded weekends because I knew it would be another weekend of being abandoned and alone. I enslaved myself into the house. What if he came home and wanted to spend time with me? I am a descent of a woman who survived the Middle Passage. How could I have enslaved myself? Every time he walked out the door, there was rejection. Every time he came back home, there was an insult to my dignity.

Another Strong Woman

In 2004, I went to the Straight Spouse Network web page and typed in, "HELP!" Michelle quickly answered. This was the first time I looked for help, and, over the next few years, I would only call Michelle the few times when things got too unbearable—though she was only an hour drive from me. I see now that she was another strong woman that God sent to me, but I did not accept it that time. I was still doing things my way.

Shanika

Things got worse between my husband and me. His drinking had gotten so bad, I feared saying anything to him. I wanted to tell the children many times. When I asked him to talk to the children, the shout I got from him was, "I will kill myself! You don't know how hard it is to be a gay black man in America today!" He was moving out of his closet; but, out of fear, I was moving deeper into it. He'd found someone he cared for, Larry, and told me he was going on a two-week cruise to Alaska with him. I asked him to move out before he went on this "trip." I felt great about that decision.

On that same day, I fell off a ladder at work and injured my back. The day I was getting my MRI, Raul and Larry were on their way to Alaska. The doctor gave me pain killers. They didn't help. I didn't tell him what was going on in my life but said I felt depressed. He sent me to a psychiatrist, and it was there I got my anti-depressant meds and sleeping pills. I was so mad that Raul went on this trip. By the time he got back, I was like the main character from the play, "The Diary of an Angry Black Woman." Most people see me as an easy going, easy to forget, and easy to forgive person, but I have this one side of me that, when pushed, can reveal a whole new side. I can be relentless. My family and friends have given this dark side of me a nickname. I have an alter ego, and her name is "Shanika."

When Raul was drinking, words came easy to him and, no matter how they pierced my heart with pain, he had no hesitation sharing. So, I decided to match him, drink to drink and word to word. I thought that I'd only fallen off a ladder onto the floor, but actually I'd fallen into Dante's Inferno. We fought so furiously that the family dogs whimpered at night. Three years is long enough to be in hell.

Did I ask him to leave? Hell, no. How would I torment him if he wasn't here? I was insane with anger. I remember one night, we were drinking and talking and he got mad and was going somewhere. I didn't want him to drive and was trying to get the keys from him. While he was getting in the car, he raised his hand to me; he'd never done that before. I stepped towards him and screamed, "Hit me! But be aware that, if you do, one or two things will happen tonight. They will be picking up one body or two bodies out of this front yard. At this point, I do not give a damn! Hit me!"

He stepped back, lowered his hand, and apologized. That night, I decided to stop drinking.

The Cry for Help

My friend Michelle from the Straight Spouse Network was always there for me, never judging. She was my gentle voice for me in my crazy place, but I still would not meet with her.

As I got off the alcohol, I began to see the light but was still doing things my way. I went home to Louisiana in 2005. It was a great trip. I went to the family church built in 1803 and sat there as the women of my past had done, praying. I felt strong and knew that I had to leave this marriage. I wanted to share with my family, but this was not the time. We were home to celebrate my godmother's 80th birthday; I did not want to make this about me. A week later, one fourth of my family was homeless from Hurricane Katrina. I knew that if I could have gotten a message to them, they would have said, "As soon as a helicopter rescues us off the roof, we will be there to help you." I truly regret not sharing from the beginning with my family.

August 2007 was a monumental month. In need of support, I called Michelle. It was time. I was desperate. She had always invited me to come and meet her or she would come and meet me. We were about 90 miles apart. It took an hour to get there and five to say goodbye. Michelle was nonjudgmental and a true objective listener. We laughed and shed a lot of tears. I knew for the first time in 20 something years, I wasn't alone.

It was also in August 2007 that our second grandchild was born. Our daughter was just getting back from the hospital. It was a Saturday, and we should have been doing grandparent stuff to get ready for the baby. Raul chose to go to work. I went to his office and was livid to find his lover there. He left Larry in his office, and we went to the park to talk. He told me, "When it comes to sex, I have no moral standards." He gave me a valium to calm me down. Then we left the park and went to our daughter's home. In the picture of me holding my new granddaughter, I looked like shit. Seeing it, I thought, "If I continue on this route, if I don't do something, I'm going to miss out on my life. I can't go on like this."

In October 2007, I found out that my support group, my life line, had a weekend event where everyone gathered together. Although reluctant, I knew I needed to be with others who really understood. I made reservations and went. The only person I knew there was Michelle. I got there on a Friday evening. Most people had already arrived. I was frightened. I didn't want to belong to this group of straight spouses. I was in denial. It made my life too real. As I met people and met the group, I thanked God for them. I went to a workshop called the Healing Circle where I heard other people's stories. It validated me. Even so, I put my head down for the group picture so I couldn't be identified. I was still in the closet then. This year will be my fifth gathering.

A few weeks later, I went to my granddaughter's baptism. I was standing at the altar and looked at the priest's eyes and said to myself, "I don't know what he has, but I know that's what I want." It was the look of love, joy, and peace. It was the first time I softened my heart to let the Holy Spirit flirt with me. I slowly returned to God and attended church, sitting way in the back like a small wild kitten afraid to go to the saucer to take a little lap of milk.

Writing this story has been very hard. I've tried to remember and write down what he said and what I said, but I cannot find the words to express the horror I felt. All my life in the happy or sad times, words will come to me in the middle of the night effortlessly. I call them my puzzle stories because I will get a piece here and there, not in any order, and, over weeks or months, I'll wake up and it all falls into place. This is the first story I've ever written down. It explains the darkness of not wanting to live, the hope for false romantic love, and the realization of the destruction he was causing my soul.

I Fell in Love with a Vampire

"I fell in love with a vampire; a cold and cutting vampire, the most dangerous kind of vampire. When he walks into a room, he instills fear into the hearts of other vampires. He learned my likes, dislikes, and fears only to keep me near. He used me as a cover not that he was concerned about what society thought of him; but, as long as he was in my world and by my side, he could deny in his heart what he truly was, a vampire. He nibbled at the very essence of my being night after night, year after year. I know not what my vampire sucked from me first, joy, laughter, love, or my very soul. But I know I was no longer the woman I once was. I do remember the last time with my vampire, that cold southern night I lay by his side. I felt a stir of life deep in the marrow of my bones. I went to the mirror to try to find some evidence of Evangeline. As I pulled closer to the mirror, I should have seen a life breath upon it, but none came from me. As I looked at the reflection of my eyes, I realized that, if I stay, that would be the last life that would ever stir within me." (Dejoie, 2012)

December 31, 2007, I demanded my husband leave and he did. He moved out. I thought he was going to live with Larry, but he stayed at a friend's apartment that happened to be unfurnished and empty for the season. We were getting ready to tell our daughter that we separated and, on January 2, her fiancé's mother died. It was not the time.

Raul courted me with phone calls, tickets to here and there, and fine dinners. It was interesting, but I heard the voice, "Be careful, Evangeline, your vampire still wants to be in your world." Mardi Gras was coming up, and we always went to Mardi Gras. I love it, and Raul, knowing this, asked if I wanted to go. I thought I would be safe, knowing I'd be with family and it was my favorite time of year, so I said "YES!" Oh! The city of New Orleans, this is the city where we fell in love and went on our honeymoon. It was hard. We passed little cafes where we had spent time. We passed Audubon Park where new lovers kissed, but the voice in me said, "Guard your heart, Evangeline. Your vampire still hunts for you." One dark moment, I thought, "Oh Raul is here with me by choice and left Larry back. Now Larry can feel the pain I have known the past years." How little did I know that eight days later Larry would commit suicide?

I pray each day for his soul. Raul was lost, and I felt that he was suicidal. He asked to come back home until he could get himself together. I opened the door and let him in.

I was searching the daily paper for Larry's obituary. That's when I lost my breath. I thought Larry was a counselor, a psychiatrist, a therapist. I never could have guessed in a million years that he was a retired priest. I had so much anger. I realized at the moment that these two men were not going to affect nor interfere with my relationship with God. I realized that I could no longer hold God accountable for what they had done. Seeing Larry's obit somehow sealed my intimate relationship with God. I shut out the world and all of its pain, knowing it was incited from the world. I was after a love unfounded. In my new life in God, I actually found I was able to cope with my family relationships better, too.

My father, who had an early onset of dementia, was coming to stay with us for six months just four days after Larry's suicide. This is my story of surrender to God.

I know we have to open ourselves up to His plan. I remember waking up mad at God that I was still here. I would have traded my life for anyone. I begged Him to take my life. Most people who saw me saw a happy functioning "Evangeline." They had no idea of the pain, suffering, or darkness.

I remember it was a beautiful March night in Florida. We were sitting on the lanai. Raul was drinking heavily. I had to give my father meds which required me to wear gloves. It was difficult. My dad was accusing me of trying to kill him, and he threw the pills on the ground.

Have you ever tried to wrestle pills from dogs? Well, I was there under the table, scrambling for those pills before my dogs got to them first... while Raul, drunk and miserable, is crying out, "I can't believe I killed Larry! I can't believe I killed Larry! I can't believe I killed Larry," so many times my dad yells out, "Who did Raul kill and who the hell is Larry?"

I'm trying to convince my dad that I'm not trying to kill him, but the meds were going to help him. Raul is crying over Larry, and the dogs are going nuts, thinking they've been scammed of treats. I calmed down my dad and put him to bed. I lay next to Raul till he stopped crying and fell asleep. I washed the dogs' mouths out, and, when everyone was calm, I went to my room, dropped to my knees, and said, "Lord, I'm in your hands. Do with me what you please." I thought I was going to get hit by lightning. In reality, that was the first night in over 20 years I slept. It was the first morning I woke up and heard the birds singing a song of celebration of me. At that point, I knew I needed spiritual counsel.

One Saturday, I went to talk to a priest. He could tell I was in a bad place and just let me talk. He realized my husband is gay and just seemed to understand. He consoled me and empathized. He validated me. Although I found peace talking to him, I needed to go to a different church because it was hard for me to go to the church where Larry had been a member and where his funeral had been. I also felt Larry's presence there and needed my own spiritual space.

So I found another church. It was late afternoon 5 pm Saturday Mass. Sundays were always bad for me. Weekends were lonely and isolating. I knew I needed to be with God instead of in a fetal position on the floor. I remember sobbing so hard that even my dogs took pity on me and would lick away my tears.

I went to confession after Mass. God had always been there waiting for me, but this was the first time I walked in with a heart ready to accept His mercy. The priest was kind and compassionate; I knew I found a home and that Father Martin would be my spiritual guide.

Father Martin

Who is Father Martin? At the time I met him, he was very young. He was just 30 and had been a priest for only 3 years. He has calmness about him and a way of making you feel the love of God. He makes things very simple. I told my story expecting to hear "You're married. Go home, pray and bear your cross." But what did I get? Compassion. "God did not intend for you to live in pain like this. Raul betrayed you on the wedding day. You walked up with your heart open, and he walked up with lies."

I asked him, "Do you think I'm crazy?"

He smiled. "No, but you live in a crazy place."

I asked him what I should do, waiting for maybe three books, 20 pamphlets and CD's, and other things. But he said, "Find your peace and joy in God." He sent me to the Adoration Chapel to sit. He gave me one reading: "Be still and know that I am God."

As I settled down, I felt the presence of the women of my past and I sat among them. I started to understand the intimacy of the love they had for their God. There was no need for words. Over time, I felt God's presence and the warmth of His hands. Slowly, He untied all the tangles, the knots, the pain, and devastation that consumed my soul.

Father Martin understood not to overwhelm me; he waited for my spirit to become stronger. He genuinely wanted to understand me. He'd never spoken to a straight spouse, and we spent hours talking. I offered him the book, The Other Side of The Closet, and was amazed he read it. As I got better, I wanted to know more about God's truth and His ways. Father Martin introduced me to another support group, wonderful people who are living the truth.

At first, every time I would see Father Martin, I would tell him, "Thank you for pulling me from the edge of the cliff. I do not see a psychiatrist nor a counselor. I am off the antidepressants and sleeping pills. You're saving me a fortune!"

His answer was always, "It's the Holy Spirit at work." He is such a humble man.

I know all of you are wondering what happened to Raul, but this story has become about Evangeline. Raul is still trying to drag me back into his crazy world. As I learned more about the truth, I realized I had to go deeper and examine my own conscience. I discovered my greatest sin was my pride. Raul always told me that he could lose himself in me, that through me he could forget his problems. I felt that my love could save him. I now see that the only way a person can be saved is through our Lord. Yes, people can help. People can guide you, but to be saved is "to lose one's self in our Lord." It was my pride to think that I could be the one to save Raul.

I wrote a short prayer.

"God, if I have molded myself into a beautiful vase where no one can see your magnificent wild flowers, then shatter me to the ground. If need be, pound me upon the ground until I am no more than dust. That way, my false self may be blown away in the wind. I beg that you sweep me up and, with your healing waters, mold me into the daughter you intend me to be. Amen."

When I shared this with Father Martin, he smiled and said, "Evangeline, you have grown," and I answered, "It's the Holy Spirit at work." We both smiled.

Every time we meet, he tells me, "Find your peace. Find your joy in God." I ask, "Is it really that simple?" He sweetly nods, "Yes."

My first granddaughter, Marie, was born on August 15. My second grandchild, Yvette, was born on December 8. These are Feast Days of the Blessed Virgin Mary. I saw this as Christ reminding me there was another strong woman from the past and to pray to His mother for strength and guidance. This deepened my faith. There has been peace and joy in my heart the last four years. I have learned to accept the love of Abba, the tenderness of Christ, the passion of the Holy Spirit; and my hope is that all will experience His joy this way.

My Children

My children are 33 and 30 now. They are successful with families of their own. I have three beautiful grandchildren with another one on the way. My daughter-in-law calls me Mom; she told me it's because it's how she feels about me in her heart. My son-in-law and I share the same birthday. He has a kind spirit. I use the terms in-law here so as to not confuse you, but in my heart I have dropped the "in-law." I have 2 sons, 2 daughters, and four grandchildren. I do believe my children benefited from having Raul and I together. He is a bad husband, but a good father. I do believe my children would have been fine if I had left this marriage. It was my choice. My children would have never asked me to stay. I pray that one day he will come out to tell his children. They love him. So, I go back to that nagging question, why do I stay?

The End of My Best Friend

About eight months ago, Raul really changed. I am sorry to say for the worst, for me. I've fallen into a dark place again. I could not say a simple child's prayer. He came out of the closet like a teenage boy just discovering his sexuality. We are still living under the same roof. At this present time, Raul has no concern about me. With all disregard, he'll call sometimes at

2:00 am, asking permission to stay out. "I've been drinking, and I should not drive."

What am I to say? "Get on the road and kill someone?" No. "Of course stay with your lover. I'm tired."

My father has just returned to stay for the next 6 months. He's asking me every five minutes, "Where's Raul?" It's driving me crazy.

Then the phone call came. It was about 11:00 pm. The guy on the line says his name is Mike. "Hi, I'm a friend of Raul's, and I think something happened to him. We were at a bar drinking. He told me he was going home, but he's not answering his phone."

My first thought was, "Maybe he's running around on you." But I decided not to be cruel.

Mike told me that Raul always talks about me and the only reason he is still alive is because of me. He tells me that Raul calls me his best friend. Tired and now worried, I told him goodnight and, if I found out anything, I'd call him back so he wouldn't worry.

I fell into the usual routine and got on the computer to look up DUI and traffic fatalities for the county. His name did not show up. I called the emergency rooms and sheriff's departments, and his name did not show up. I had to get to bed. It was late. I had to work the next day. I was exhausted. I called a person I felt was Raul's present lover. This was so humiliating. Alvin and I talked, and he told me that he could hear in my voice how worried I was. He said that if Raul was there he would tell me. He and Raul had parted paths. Raul was running with a fast drinking group, and he could not take it anymore. He mentioned that Raul had told him that I had returned to God. I told him yes that is where I found my peace. We talked a long time about him going back to God to find his peace. I was tired and said, "Goodnight. God Bless you. I will keep you in my prayers."

Raul came in the next morning looking fresh and well rested. I was exhausted and disgusted. The words, "Raul says you're his best friend" kept echoing in my mind. I've decided that I don't want to be his best friend anymore. Friends don't treat each other this way.

The Monkey and the Coconut

This has been hard for me. I just realized that tonight is one day after my daughter's 30th birthday, 4 days before my 35th wedding anniversary, and 14 days before my 56th birthday and I must finish this. In order to finish this, I've had to learn how to love my husband unconditionally. About four months ago, I shared one of my puzzle stories with Father Martin, the first person I ever shared a story with. If you recall, puzzle stories are those I remember in bits and pieces. Through dreams I can sometimes piece together these stories weeks even months later, but this one had no ending. He said that he felt that the Holy Spirit was guiding me and wanted me to listen. About two months later, he called one late Saturday afternoon and asked me to be at 9:00 am Mass. I figured I must have done something terribly wrong. In the three years I've known him, He's never asked me to attend a specific Mass. After hanging up, I did a quick examination of conscience and couldn't find any sins he would know about. So, I went to Mass. When he began his homily, I realized he'd remembered the puzzle story I'd shared with him, the one that had no end.

Listening to his homily, I realized that I was that monkey. I was that poor creature not knowing how to escape, not knowing how to let go. After I began writing this story, I woke one night and knew how the puzzle story ended. I was holding on tightly to that orange that I knew would taste so sweet and I heard a voice say, "Evangeline, let go." I tried to use all the reasoning and fears of my past.

"But I will lose my house."

"Let go of material things, and one day you will be in My Father's house with Me."

"But I will lose my beautiful garden."

"Let go, and I will bring you flowers."

"But people will see me as the liar that I am."

"Let go of your pride, and people will love you for your true self."

"But I worry about my children."

"Let go of control. Your children are a gift to you from Me. Entrust them in my hands."

"I fear for Raul."

"Let go of him. Raul will need to find his own way."

"But I want to be loved by a man the way you intended a woman to be loved."

"Let go of want. Evangeline, let me ask you this, could My love for you be enough?"

My heart whispered, "Yes."

"Evangeline, let go."

The Holy Spirit fell upon me. Every muscle softened and submitted to His will. My hand fell limp. I let the orange go. At the moment of freedom, I leapt to the top of the forest canopy. There awaiting me was a starry sky. I was no longer in the dark. My spirit was free. I saw new and sweet possibilities.

* * *

And now, Carlos, who is still living with his wife and happy. He described his transformation in a panel presentation given at a national conference of social activists in 2007.

"Seven years ago," he began, "I would not have seen myself working as a volunteer or patronizing gay and lesbian events, traveling over a thousand miles to participate in a discussion panel at a national Gay and Lesbian Task Force convention.

"Seven years ago, I would not have met many of the friends and acquaintances that now fill a great part of my life.

"Seven years ago, I would not have comprehended the struggles of mixed-orientation couples, even if I had known they existed.

"Seven years ago, I would not have the understanding I have of the gay and lesbian community as I do today.

"Seven years ago, I would not have appreciated the value of diversity, all diversity.

"Seven years ago, I would not have pondered about writing this.

"Seven years, ago, my wife of thirty years told me she was a lesbian.

"Seven years in the future… what will they bring?"

(Fernandez, 2007)

Afterword: Seen and Heard

As R. L. and I gathered the stories and vignettes you've just read, we were unprepared for the range of emotions, experiences, conflicts, and epiphanies that flooded our minds and hearts. I, Amity, was particularly blown away by the complexities of the situations they faced, the depth of their pain, the flash of their insights, and the obstacles they had to overcome at home, work, at church or temple, in the community, and inside themselves. By the time we'd read a batch of narratives or had completed a few interviews, each of us felt utterly exhausted from living vicariously through their solo struggles. R. L. says she often "tunneled back" to very dark times throughout the writing of this book. She says it affected the way in which she related to her family, friends, and the love of her life. With family and friends, she found she didn't talk much about this as she didn't feel anyone would "get it"; and, with the love in her life, she often needed the very distance she had, which, in turn, made her unable to "give" emotionally and unable to nurture the relationship. She was unprepared for the defensive walls that seemed to construct overnight. Now, however, the walls are slowly crumbling, brick by brick. "I'm feeling more like my 'now' self again."

We were struck, too, by the thrust of the narratives. Though many spouses were angry and in pain and some still are, their primary purpose for sharing was less to vent or judge, than to simply "tell," explain, describe, educate, and share their experience from their perspective.

Now that we've opened the windows on these remarkable women and men for you to see and hear, it's our hope that you, too, were able to experience their feelings, thoughts, and actions as they crafted their individual paths -- all forty plus of them from every walk of life. This multicolored picture of straight spouses' journeys, expressed in their own words, adds an important piece that helps complete the picture puzzle of our diverse society: the heretofore invisible women and men married or once married to an estimated over two million gay, lesbian, bisexual or transgender persons with whom they co-parent at least 3,500,000 children. (Buxton, 1994, 2012).

Beyond these individual narratives, it's helpful to see them in the context of all spouses whose partners have come out or are found out in mixed-orientation or trans/non-trans marriages. In respect to post-disclosure mixed-orientation couples, given the scant statistics available, the outcome of their marriages seems to break down into three broad categories. A third break up quickly because the gay, lesbian, or bisexual spouse wants to begin his or her new life or the straight spouse is angry at the deceit or infidelity or considers same-sex orientation to be immoral. Another third stay together for about a year to sort things out and then decide to separate and divorce. The final third commit to making the marriage work under the new circumstances. After about three years, half of these couples, (a sixth of the total), separate; and the other half continue their marriages, in diverse forms: monogamous, celibate, a secondary relationship with another married husband or wife, open for both partners, or polyamorous. (Buxton, 2006a). Sadly, not much is known about the outcomes for post-disclosure trans/non-trans couples.

The spouses you have seen and heard are players in the context of larger society, too, and also in the reciprocal process that exists between writer and reader.

First, the seeing part. Their experience and that of other straight spouses can be seen as an untold chapter of Gay Liberation, the movement sparked by the Stonewall Inn Riot of 1969 that enabled more closeted gay men and lesbians to be true to themselves and come out. For those in traditional marriages, their disclosure or their spouses' discovery of the hitherto unknown sexual mismatch caused pain for the straight spouses, making them in effect unintended victims of the same homophobia and heterosexism that caused their mates to marry someone of the opposite sex in the first place. This unintended consequence is repeated each time a spouse in a heterosexual marriage turns out to be gay, lesbian, bisexual, or transgender. For those who dare not come out yet are discovered, their straight wives and husbands have a doubly hard time to be seen.

Then, there's the hearing part. As reader, you opened your ears to hear the voices of spouses as they recounted the unique details of their struggles. We hope their words helped you understand the traumatic nature of unexpectedly finding out that one's husband or wife is not straight or not the gender presented. The turbulent emotions and conflicts that result go beyond those of ordinary marital problems.

Having others minimize, not understand, or ignore the depth of this existential crisis adds fuel to trauma's fire. In contrast, you paid attention and listened to the spouses' own words. That has helped them. In fact, you've just been part of the process of helping and being helped and its reciprocal benefits. Each spouse who contributed to this book knows its readers are now aware of the details of her or his journey. That is a huge gift to someone who feels isolated and devalued. At the same time, according to recent brain research of neuroscientists and psychologists, the helping gift works the other way, too. One area of our brains is actually wired for feelings of happiness or joy when triggered by social contact. Moreover, social contact with someone stuck in a negative state can often bring about his or her recovery more effectively than pills. Just as important, joy or happiness occurs as much for the person who helps someone trapped in pain, depression, anger, fear, or any negative emotion as for the person trapped. Therefore, you, the reader, whether or not you sensed you were helping the spouses whose stories you were reading, your hearing what they said and sending them empathy -- simply by being interested enough to read -- helped each of them heal a little bit more. Now that you know how you have helped them, we hope you, in turn, feel some degree of happiness or joy from this reading experience.

We leave you with deep gratitude for tuning into these persons' lives and with hope that you might carry this seen and heard knowledge into your everyday life, whether to acknowledge a straight spouse you happen to meet or whether to become vocal in informing others about the unintended consequences of societal and religious perceptions of "normalcy" or morality that makes some people try to cure or change the same-sex orientation of gay, lesbian, and bisexual persons and exert pressure on them to marry opposite-sex partners as the right thing to do, or try to keep transgender persons from expressing their real gender identity.

Most of all, we hope that you've gained in understanding and appreciation of the resiliency of the human spirit and the power of individual discernment, integrity, and courage that these women and men shared. Thank you for joining us on our journey.

A last word from Lewis, who emailed his fellow straight spouses a key question and composed a poem in answer — something for you to ponder as you walk in memory with the men and women in this book.

"I've been thinking about the amazing accomplishment many of you have done: totally awesome strength and character. Even though your spouse left you or left you emotionally, you keep going. For some, poverty, depression, loneliness, passionless, nobody to help. Like those who are poor and worrying about the next utility to be shut off — you keep going. Like those who are left alone with children and teens who just do not get it — you keep going. But you are still a mother. A father. Like those men devastated by emotional pain who still get up and try to save their jobs, yet also try to be a father to unappreciative teens or a single father to young ones. Those who lose homes, yet find a place to live.

"And here is the ugly reality: nobody is there to celebrate your awesome character and strength. That is why we are here. So, here's a poem for you, and for me."

Who is there to celebrate?
Who is there to commend?
Who is there to admire,
To say, "Job well done."?
Not your love. Gone.
Not your children. Young.
Who understands?
That one who was close and there,
now doesn't speak, is absent.
Silent.

Family, friends, they don't see or know.
Who is there to celebrate, to commend and to admire?
Few can even take note of your strength.
None can understand your stamina.
Nobody sees you get up when down.
Where is he who can understand your labor?
All that you do, all that you have done?
Who is there to celebrate?
You.

Say, "Wow, I did great things.
Even in the midst of horror and shock,
in hopelessness and confusion.
Although left in the rubble of separation,
I did the outstanding and remarkable, like
Simply --
Staying,
Caring,
Working,
Nurturing,
Being with,

Continuing,
Hoping,
Breathing."

Celebrate!
You are amazing!
You are held in high regard.
You who just keep going.

References and Resources

References (Some are used in this book; others are for further reading.)

Aesop. (Sixth century, BC). Fables, in The Harvard Classics, 1909-14.

Barbetta, F. (2008). A pebble in his shoe: The diary of a straight spouse. Pennsylvania: Dr. Francine Barbetta.

Bukowsky, C. Retrieved from http://www.goodreads.com/quotes/show/54579.

Buxton, A. (2012). Straight husbands whose wives come out: Challenges to the myth of masculinity. *Journal of GLBT Family Studies*, 8(1) (January-February), 23-45.

Buxton, A. (2011b). A crisis of faith: When a spouse comes out. In J. Schexnayder, Setting the table: Preparing Catholic parishes to welcome lesbian, gay, bisexual, and transgender people and their families (pp. 116-21). Berkeley, CA: Catholic Association for Lesbian and Gay Ministry.

Buxton, A. (2011a). Reflections on bisexuality through the prism of mixed-orientation marriages. *Journal of Bisexuality*, 1(4), 525-544.

Buxton, A. (2007). Counseling heterosexual spouses of bisexual or transgender partners. In B. Firestein (Ed.), Becoming visible: Counseling bisexuals across the lifespan (pp. 635-665). New York, NY: Columbia University Press.

Buxton, A. (2006d). When a spouse comes out: Impact on the heterosexual spouse. *Sexual addiction & compulsivity: Journal of treatment and prevention (Sexual addiction and the family, special issue),* 13(2-3), 317-332.

Buxton, A. (2006c). Counseling heterosexual spouses and bisexual-heterosexual couples: An affirmative approach. In R. C. Fox (Ed.), Affirmative psychotherapy with bisexual women and bisexual men (pp. 105-135). New York, NY: Harrington Park Press.

Buxton, A. (2006b). Healing an invisible minority: How the Straight Spouse Network has become the prime source of support for those in mixed-orientation marriages. In J. J. Bigner and A. R. Gottlieb (Eds.), Interventions with families of gay, lesbian, bisexual, and transgender people: From the inside out (pp. 46-69). New York, NY: Harrington Park Press.

Buxton, A. (2006a). A family matter: When a spouse comes out as gay, lesbian, or bisexual. *Journal of GLBT Family Studies*, 9(2), 49-70.

Buxton, A. (2004b) Paths and pitfalls: How heterosexual spouses cope when their husbands or wives come out. *Journal of couple & relationship therapy*, 3 (2/3), 95-109.

Buxton, A. (2004a). Works in progress: How mixed-orientation couples maintain their marriages after the wives come out. In R. C. Fox (Ed.), Current Research in Bisexuality (pp. 57-82). New York, NY: Haworth Press.

Buxton, A. (2001). Writing our own script: How bisexual men and their heterosexual wives maintain their marriages after disclosure. In B. Beemyn and E. Steinman (Eds.), Facts and fictions: Experiencing male bisexuality (pp. 157-189). New York, NY: Haworth Press.

Buxton, A. (2000) From hostile to helpful. In J Wells (Ed.), Home fronts: Controversies in nontraditional parenting (pp. 201-11). New York, NY: Alyson Press.

Buxton, A. (1999). The best interest of children of gay and lesbian parents, in R. Galatzer-Levy and L. Kraus (Eds.), The scientific basis of child custody decisions, first edition (pp.313-46). New York, NY: John Wiley & Sons.

Buxton, A. (1994). The other side of the closet: The coming-out crisis for straight spouses and families, revised and expanded. New York, NY: John Wiley & Sons.

Buxton, A. (1991). The other side of the closet: The coming-out crisis for straight spouses. Santa Monica, CA: IBS Press.

DeJoie. E. (2012). Personal journal.

Fernandez, C. (2007). Presentation, Creating Change Conference, Gay and Lesbian Task Force.

Gochros, J. (1989). When husbands come out of the closet. New York, NY: Harrington Park Press.

Grever, C. (2001). My husband is gay. Santa Cruz, CA: Crossing Press.

Grever, C. and Bowman, D. (2007). When a spouse comes out: A straight mate's recovery manual. New York, NY: Haworth Press.

Komuves, L. C. (2006). Silent sagas: Unsung sorrows. (pdf ebook) IUniverse.

Maslow, A. Retrieved from http:www./thinkexist.com/quotation/but behavior in the human being is sometimes a/154449.html

Roller, E. M. (2010). On thundering wings: Homosexuality, love & the church on trial. Winterset, IA: Golden Tree Communications.

Selig, J. (2012). Story of my marriage falling apart: Dealing with depression and coming out. http://www.johnselig.com/podcast/2012/02/19/episode-81-john-seig-outspoken-the-book-one-person-at-a-time-a-coming-out-chronicle/

Straight Spouse Network. (2007). Spouses of transgender partners, 101. Available: information@straightspouse.org

Straight Spouse Network. (2006). You're not alone. Retrieved from http://www.straightspouse.org/personalstories.php

Straight Spouse Network. (2005). Out together. Retrieved from http://www.straightspouse.org/personalstories.php

Resources

The Straight Spouse Network puts straight spouses and mixed-orientation or transgender/non-transgender couples worldwide in touch with one another through support groups (face-to-face and online), regional gatherings, and individual contacts. The Network also provides research-based information on all aspects of mixed-orientation or trans/nontrans marriages and family issues to increase understanding between spouses, within families, and with the larger community, especially professionals. (See References)

PO Box 507, Mahwah, NJ 07430
201-825-7763 or information@straightspouse.org
www.straightspouse.org

COLAGE provides information, support, personal contacts, and programs for children who have a lesbian, gay, bisexual, or transgender parent.

4509 Interlake Ave., N #180, Seattle, WA 98103
855-4-COLAGE or colage@colage.org
www.colage.org

Family Equality Council (FEC) supports, connects, and represents gay, lesbian, bisexual, and transgender parents and the children they are raising.

PO Box 206, Boston, MA 02133
617-502-8700
www.familyequality.org

Parents, Families, and Friends of Lesbians and Gays (PFLAG) provides direct support, education, and advocacy programs regarding sexual orientation and gender identity, offering opportunities for dialogue and acting to create a society that is healthy and respectful of human diversity. Chapters are located throughout the United States.

1726 M Street, NW, Suite 400, Washington, DC 20036
202-467-8180 or info@pflag.org
www.pflag.org

About the Authors

Amity Pierce Buxton, her Ph.D. from Columbia University, has taught grades pre-school through graduate school. Member of the American Psychological Association, she serves on the editorial boards of the Journal of Bisexuality and the Journal of GLBT Family Studies and on the board of the Catholic Association for Gay and Lesbian Ministry. She wrote The Other Side of the Closet: the Coming-Out Crisis for Straight Spouses and Families and founded the worldwide Straight Spouse Network. Currently, she counsels spouses and couples, conducts research, writes articles and chapters, lectures, and gives workshops on all aspects of the impact of a spouse's coming out in a mixed-orientation or transgender/non-transgender marriage.

R. L. Pinely

Being a widow would have been easier than grieving the loss of my marriage. Why? When a loved one passes, there's closure. When I discovered my spouse was gay, I was imprisoned in a very deep dark closet for a very long time. I stayed there and suffocated. It was during my darkest moments that I renewed my faith, listened to my inner voice, and found an unyielding strength I never knew I had. Slowly, I started to create the life I knew I deserved and freed myself. Many years have passed, and now my life takes on a whole new definition. When I look back on it, I compare it to a field after a fire: there's new growth. Through faith alone, my life's being rebuilt, one day at a time.

Collaborating with Amity to write this book has been an amazing journey. Absorbing her expertise has been a rare privilege as we lived vicariously through the lives of others and walked in their shoes. As owner of an online support group, I'm so thankful that I have the opportunity every day to pass along her wisdom, insight, experience, and understanding to nearly 3,000 women.

If I had a message to impart, it would be to love yourself enough to lead the life you know you're meant to live. The most important relationship we can nurture is the one within ourselves. If we can't unconditionally love ourselves, we can't possible love another. Sometimes the most difficult choices with which we're faced are the ones that can set us free.

The Journey continues.
R. L. Pinely

CPSIA information can be obtained at www.ICGtesting.com
Printed in the USA
BVOW01s1204011014

369054BV00001B/248/P